Annabel **Karmel's**
NEW COMPLETE
Baby and Toddler
Meal Planner

Annabel **Karmel's**
NEW COMPLETE
Baby and Toddler Meal Planner

Over 200 quick, easy and healthy recipes

ANNABEL KARMEL

Illustrations by Nadine Wickenden

EBURY PRESS
LONDON

7 9 10 8 6

Published in 2007 by Ebury Press, an imprint of
Ebury Publishing

A Random House Group Company

The Random House Group Limited Reg. No. 954009

Addresses for companies within the Random House Group
can be found at www.randomhouse.co.uk

A CIP catalogue record for this book is available from
the British Library

The Random House Group Limited makes every effort to
ensure that the papers used in our books are made from
trees that have been legally sourced from well-managed
and credibly certified forests. Our paper procurement policy
can be found on www.randomhouse.co.uk

To buy books by your favourite authors and register for
offers visit www.rbooks.co.uk

Printed and bound in China by C&C Offset Printing Co., Ltd.

ISBN 9780091900311

*This book is dedicated
to my children,
Nicholas, Lara and Scarlett,
and to the memory of
my first daughter,
Natasha.*

CONTENTS

INTRODUCTION

Like any other besotted young mother, I wanted the very best for my babies. As a food lover and cordon bleu cook, I wanted them to enjoy the wonderful tastes and aromas of fresh foods. With common sense, extensive research, cooperative infants and a tolerant husband I knew I could create delicious recipes. Prepared quickly and easily they would be better for babies and toddlers than commercial vitamin- and iron-fortified powders and bland processed purées with a shelf-life of over two years.

Poor nutrition can cause problems that will plague our children for the rest of their lives. A recent government study found that as many as two-thirds of cancer cases are linked to the type of food that people eat. The untimely death of my first child Natasha at the age of thirteen weeks was the catalyst that spurred me into writing this book, which has now become such a valuable and popular, practical guide to parents all over the world.

Battles over the dinner table are one of the more dubious pleasures of parenthood. Blessed is the mother who has never encountered the tenacious iron will of a child who will not eat. I now have three children and the pleasure of seeing them enjoy my foods has been a wonderful experience. I am reassured to know that they are eating good fresh produce not over-processed convenience foods.

At a time when diet is most crucial to our child's health, why should most meals emanate from jars and packets? There is no great mystique to making your own baby food, and nothing can be better than home-cooked purées made from good-quality fresh, natural ingredients. Don't be overwhelmed by the impressive lists of nutritional information on the labels of commercial baby foods: your own will contain the same goodness but without any added starches (like maltodextrin, which is the same substance that provides the glue on envelopes and stamps!).

Not only do home-made purées taste like real food, they also work out much cheaper. Even busy working mums can give their baby the best start in life, since foods like mashed banana, avocado and papaya make excellent no-cook baby purées. You can plan your baby's menus ahead and, in just a couple of hours, prepare a whole month's food supply for your baby, freezing extra portions in ice-cube trays. You can also turn many baby purées into delicious soups for the rest of the household by adding stock and seasoning, and many family meals such as a chicken casserole with vegetables can be suitable for your baby if you set aside a portion and cook it without salt or spices.

In early childhood, eating habits and tastes (good or bad) are formed for life, so by introducing your baby to a wide range of fresh, stimulating flavours you will help establish a healthy eating pattern. Commercial carrot purées always taste the same, but with home-made purées babies get used to the natural variations in the taste of home-cooked food, which helps them to adapt to family meals as they grow up.

I give feeding guidelines, but there are no hard and fast rules since every baby develops at his or her own pace. Children need calories to grow as well as an adequate supply of proteins, vitamins and minerals. This is best provided by a good varied diet. Although a low-fat, high-fibre diet is fine for adults, it is not appropriate for young children. Babies should not have salt added to their food, but salt in moderation after one year is unlikely to do any harm.

If there are rules – and rules are made to be broken – they are to aim for:

- Fresh food
- Low animal fat
- Low sugar
- Low salt (no salt before one year).

A baby in the home is an opportunity to look at the dietary rules for the whole family. Some of these recipes are so delicious I serve them when entertaining! Babies' nutrition in their first year probably has a greater influence than at any other time of life. This reinforces the need to start early with a good balanced diet. When your child opts for the raw fruits and vegetables (which adults imagine kids hate) over sugary sweets, you will recognise your success.

Good luck. I hope you and your child enjoy many happy meals together!

CHAPTER ONE

THE BEST FIRST FOODS FOR YOUR BABY

The UK Department of Health guidelines (May 2003) recommend breast-feeding exclusively for the first six months, as this should meet all your baby's nutritional needs. Most babies shouldn't need solid foods before the age of six months, but if you feel that yours does need them earlier, speak to your health visitor or GP. Signs that your baby may be ready are if he is still hungry after a full milk feed, demands more frequent feeds or wakes at night for a feed having previously slept through. There's no 'right' age to introduce solids as every baby is different. However, it's important that you don't wean him too early (not before seventeen weeks) as his digestive system won't fully mature for the first few months, and foreign proteins very early on may increase the likelihood of food allergies later.

MILK IS STILL THE MAJOR FOOD

It is very important to remember, when starting your baby on solids, that milk is still the best and most natural food for growing babies. I would encourage mothers to give breastfeeding a try. Apart from the emotional benefits, breast milk contains antibodies that will help protect infants from infection. In the first few months, they are particularly vulnerable and the colostrum a mother produces in the first few days of breastfeeding is a very important source of antibodies which help to build up a baby's immune system. (If only for this reason, it is obvious that there are some enormous benefits in breastfeeding your child, even for as little as one week.) It is also medically proven that breastfed babies are less likely to develop certain diseases in later life.

Milk should contain all the nutrients your baby needs to grow. There are 65 calories in 120 ml/4 fl oz milk, and formula milk is fortified with vitamins and iron. Cow's milk isn't such a 'complete' food for human babies so is best not started until your baby is one year old. Solids are introduced to add *bulk* to a baby's diet, and to introduce new tastes, textures and aromas; they also help the baby to practise using the muscles in his mouth. But giving a baby too much solid food too early may lead to constipation, and provide fewer nutrients than he needs. It would be very difficult for a baby to get the equivalent amount of nutrients from the small amount of solids he will consume as he gets from his milk.

Don't use softened water or repeatedly boiled water when making up your baby's bottle, because of the danger of concentrating mineral salts. Babies' bottles should not be warmed in a microwave, as the milk may be too hot even though the bottle feels cool to the touch. Warm bottles by standing them in hot water.

Between four and six months babies should have 600–800 ml/21–28 fl oz breast or infant formula each day. 600 ml/21 fl oz is enough when solids are introduced but it isn't between four and six months with no solids. It's important to make sure that, up to the age of eight months, your baby drinks milk at least four times a day (especially as it is highly likely that a bottle may not be finished at each feed). If the number of feeds is reduced too quickly, your baby will not be able to drink as much as is needed. Some mothers make the mistake of giving their baby solid food when he is hungry, when what he really needs is an additional milk feed.

Babies should be given breast or formula milk for the whole of the first year. Ordinary cow's, goat's or sheep's milk is not suitable as your baby's main drink as it doesn't contain enough iron and other nutrients for proper growth. However, whole cow's milk can be used in cooking or with cereal when weaning. Dairy products like yoghurt, fromage frais and cheese can be introduced once first tastes of fruit and vegetables are accepted and are generally very popular with babies. Choose full-fat products as opposed to low-fat as babies need the calories for proper growth.

FRESH IS BEST

Fresh foods just do taste, smell and look better than jars of pre-prepared baby foods. Nor is there any doubt that, prepared correctly, they are better for your baby (and you), for it is inevitable that nutrients, especially vitamins, are lost in the processing of pre-prepared baby foods. Home-made foods taste different from the jars you can buy. I believe your child will be less fussy and find the transition to joining in with family meals easier if he is used to a wide selection of fresh tastes and textures from an early age.

ORGANIC

Organic fruit and vegetables are produced without artificial chemicals, such as pesticides and fertilisers. However, there is at present no scientific evidence that pesticide levels in ordinary foods are harmful to young babies and children, but some mothers prefer not to take the risk. It is an environmentally friendly option but generates higher prices and it is up to you to decide whether it's worth the extra money.

GM FOODS

Genetic modification (GM) is the process of transferring genes from one species to another. For example, a tendency to resist frost or damage from certain insects could be implanted from one plant to another. More research is needed to know whether genetic modification can improve the quality and availability of crops or whether the cost to humans and the environment outweigh any benefit. If you wish to avoid GM foods, consult the labels as by 2005 it will be compulsory to declare if any GM ingredients are present.

NUTRITIONAL REQUIREMENTS
Proteins

Proteins are needed for the growth and repair of our bodies; any extra can be used to provide energy (or is deposited as fat). Proteins are made up of different amino acids. Some foods (meat, fish, soya beans and dairy produce, including cheeses) contain all the amino acids that are essential to our bodies. Other foods (grains, pulses, nuts and seeds) are valuable sources of protein but don't contain all the essential amino acids.

Carbohydrates

Carbohydrates and fat provide our bodies with their main source of energy. There are two types of carbohydrate: sugar and starch (which in complex form provides fibre). In both types there are two forms: natural and refined. The natural form provides a more healthy alternative.

SUGARS	
Natural	Fruits and fruit juices
	Vegetables and vegetable juices
Refined	Sugars and honey
	Soft drinks
	Sweet jellies
	Jams and other preserves
	Biscuits and cakes
STARCHES	
Natural	Wholegrain breakfast cereals, flour, bread and pasta
	Brown rice
	Potatoes
	Dried beans and lentils
	Peas, bananas and many other fruits and vegetables
Refined	Processed breakfast cereals (e.g. sugar-coated flakes)
	White flour, breads and pasta
	White rice
	Sugary biscuits and cakes

Fats

Fats provide the most concentrated source of energy, and babies need proportionately more fat in their diet than adults. Energy-dense foods like cheese, meat and eggs are needed to fuel their rapid growth and development, and fat provides more than 50 per cent of the energy in breast milk. Foods that contain fats also contain fat soluble vitamins A, D, E and K, which are important for the healthy development of your baby. The problem is that many people eat too much fat and the wrong type.

There are two types of fat – saturated (solid at room temperature) which mainly come from animal sources and from artificially hardened fats found in cakes, biscuits and hard margarines, and unsaturated (liquid at room temperature), which come from vegetable sources. It is the saturated fats which are the most harmful and which may lead to high cholesterol levels and coronary disease later in life.

It is important to give your baby whole milk for at least the first two years but try to reduce fats in cooking and use butter and margarine in moderation. Try to reduce saturated fats in your child's diet by cutting down on fatty meats like fatty minced meat or sausages and replace them with lean red meat, chicken or oily fish.

Essential fatty acids are important for your baby's brain and visual development. There are two types of EFA omega 3 from seed oils eg: sunflower, safflower and corn, and omega 6 from oily fish eg: salmon, trout, sardines and fresh tuna. In general we get enough omega 3 in our diets – it is the omega 6 that is often low. The right balance of both types of EFAs are important, especially in early life.

Vitamins and Minerals

For most babies who eat fresh food in sufficient quantities and drink formula milk until the age of one year, vitamin supplements are probably unnecessary. However, in the UK the Department of Health recommends that if your baby is being breastfed (breastmilk doesn't contain enough Vitamin D) or is drinking less than 500 ml/18 fl oz of infant formula a day, you should give him vitamin supplements from the age of six months to two years. Ask your health visitor for advice.

Children following a vegan diet should have at least 600 ml/21 fl oz of a fortified infant soya milk daily until the age of two, then they won't need supplements. It is mainly Vitamins A and D that are likely to be low in children aged six months to two years who don't have 500 ml/18 fl oz fortified infant or soya formula.

Vitamins are necessary for the correct development of the brain and nervous system. A good balanced diet should supply all the nutrients your child needs and an excess of vitamins is potentially harmful, but children who are picky eaters could benefit by taking a multi-vitamin supplement specially designed for children.

There are two types of vitamins – water-soluble (C and B complex) and fat-soluble (A, D, E and K). Water-soluble vitamins cannot be stored by the body, so foods containing these should be eaten daily. They can also easily be destroyed by overcooking, especially when fruits and vegetables are boiled in water. You should try to preserve these vitamins by eating the foods raw or just lightly cooked (in a steamer, for instance).

VITAMIN A

Essential for growth, healthy skin, tooth enamel and good vision.

Liver
Oily fish
Carrots
Dark green leafy vegetables (e.g. broccoli)
Sweet potatoes
Squash
Tomatoes
Apricots and mangoes

VITAMIN B COMPLEX

Essential for growth, for changing food into energy, for a healthy nervous system and as an aid to digestion. There are a large number of vitamins in the B group. Some are found in many foods, but no foods except for liver and yeast extract contain them all.

Meat
Sardines
Dairy produce and eggs
Wholegrain cereals
Dark green vegetables
Yeast extract (e.g. Marmite)
Nuts
Dried beans
Bananas

VITAMIN C

Needed for growth, healthy tissue and healing of wounds. It helps in the absorption of iron.
Vegetables such as: broccoli,
sweet peppers, potatoes, spinach,
cauliflower
Fruits such as: citrus fruits, blackcurrants,
melon, papaya, strawberries, kiwi fruit

VITAMIN D

Essential for proper bone formation, it works in conjunction with calcium. It's found in few foods, but is made by the skin in the presence of sunlight.
Oily fish
Eggs
Margarine
Dairy produce

VITAMIN E

Important for the composition of the cell structure. Helps the body create and maintain red blood cells.
Vegetable oils
Avocado
Wheatgerm
Nuts and seeds

CALCIUM

Important for strong bones, good teeth and growth.
Dairy products
Canned fish with bones (e.g. sardines)
Dried fruit
White bread
Green leafy vegetables
Pulses

IRON

Needed for healthy blood and muscles. Iron deficiency is very common and will leave your child feeling tired and run down. Red meat is the best source of iron.
Red meat, especially liver
Oily fish
Egg yolks
Dried fruits (especially apricots)
Wholegrain and fortified cereals
Lentils and dried beans
Green leafy vegetables

High-Risk Foods

More and more children are developing an allergy to sesame seeds, so don't give them to highly atopic babies until they're at least nine months. Berry and citrus fruits can trigger a reaction but rarely cause a true allergy. The most common allergic problems that may be triggered by an adverse reaction to food are: nausea; vomiting; diarrhoea; asthma; eczema; hayfever; rashes and swelling of the eyes, lips and face. This is one reason why it's unwise to rush starting your baby on solid foods.

POTENTIAL HIGH-RISK FOODS
Cow's milk and dairy produce
Nuts and seeds
Eggs
Wheat-based products
Fish (especially shellfish)
Chocolate

Water

Humans can survive for quite a time without food, but only a few days without water. Babies lose more water through their skin and kidneys than adults and also through vomiting and diarrhoea. Thus it's vital that they don't become dehydrated. Ensure your baby drinks plenty of fluids; cool, boiled water is the best drink to give on hot days – it's a better thirst quencher than any sugary drink. Avoid bottled mineral water as it can contain high concentrations of mineral salts, which are unsuitable for babies.

It really isn't necessary to give a very young baby anything to drink other than milk or plain water if he is just thirsty. Fruit syrups, squashes and sweetened herbal drinks should be discouraged, to prevent dental decay. Don't be fooled if the packet says 'dextrose' – this is just a type of sugar.

If your baby refuses to drink water, then give him unsweetened baby juice or fresh 100 per cent fruit juice. Dilute according to instructions or, for fresh juice, use one part juice to three parts water.

THE QUESTION OF ALLERGIES

If your family has a history of food allergy or atopic disease such as hayfever, asthma or eczema, there is an increased risk of developing an allergic disorder, so foods should be introduced with great care. If possible, breastfeed exclusively for the first six months. If not, discuss with your doctor the option of using a 'hypoallergenic' infant formula instead. When weaning, start with low allergen foods like baby rice, root vegetables, apple or pear. New foods should be introduced one at a time and tried for two or three days. In that way, if there is a reaction you will know what has caused it. Avoid high-risk foods until your baby is nine to twelve months old.

There's no need to worry about food allergies unless there is a family history of allergy or atopic disease. The incidence of food allergy in normal babies is very small and, with the tendency to a later introduction of solid food at six months, they've become even less common. Don't remove key foods like milk and wheat from your child's diet before consulting a doctor. Many children grow out of their allergies by the age of two, but some – particularly a sensitivity to eggs, milk, nuts or shellfish – can last for life. If your child has an allergy, tell any adults who may feed him.

Never be afraid to take your baby to the doctor if you are worried that something is wrong. Young babies' immune systems aren't fully matured and babies can become ill very quickly if they aren't treated properly and can develop serious complications.

Lactose Intolerance

Lactose intolerance isn't actually an allergy but the inability to digest lactose – the sugar in milk – because of a lack of a digestive enzyme. This can be hereditary and, if this is the case, your child may experience nausea, cramps, bloating, diarrhoea and gas, usually about 30 minutes after consuming dairy foods, and should be given a special diet that avoids all dairy products. Since lactose is present in breast and cow's milk, babies who are lactose intolerant should be given soya formula. However, soya milk isn't recommended for babies under the age of six months, and so these babies should be given a special low-lactose infant formula (sometimes labelled 'LF').

Lactose intolerance is a rare complication that can occur after a gastro intestinal infection. In children over one year, it's safe to remove milk products for a few days to see if this makes a difference. In babies under a year, continue to breastfeed but, if additional feeds are needed, talk to a doctor, health visitor or pharmacist about using a low-lactose feed for a couple of weeks.

If children suffer from lactose intolerance due to a lack of lactase, this will last for life.

Cow's Milk Protein Allergy

If you think your baby is sensitive to cow's milk, you should consult your doctor. Breast milk is the best alternative, but mothers should limit their own consumption of dairy products as they can be transferred to their baby through breast milk. If breastfeeding has ceased, your doctor will recommend an extensively hydrolysed (low-allergen) infant formula, which is available on prescription.

This condition means that no dairy products are tolerated. Milk-free vegetable or soya margarine may be substituted for butter. There are also many soya-based (non-dairy) yoghurts and desserts available and carob can be substituted for milk chocolate. Babies *often outgrow this allergy* by the age of two, but until then it's important to ensure your child gets enough calcium in his diet.

Eggs

Eggs can be given from six months but they must be thoroughly cooked until both the white and the yolk are solid. Soft-boiled eggs can be given after one year.

Fruits

Some children have an adverse reaction to citrus, berries and kiwi fruit. Rosehip and blackcurrant, being rich in Vitamin C, make good alternatives to orange juice.

Honey

Honey should not be given to children under twelve months as it can cause infant botulism. Although this is very rare, it is best to be safe as a baby's digestive system is too immature to deal with the bug.

Nuts

It is rare to be allergic to tree nuts such as walnuts and hazelnuts. However, peanuts and peanut products can induce a severe allergic reaction – anaphylactic shock – which can be life threatening, so it's best to be cautious. In families with a history of any allergy including hayfever, eczema and asthma, it's advisable to avoid all products containing peanuts, including peanut oil, until the child is three years old, and then seek medical advice before introducing peanut products into the diet.

Peanut butter and finely ground nuts, however, can be introduced from six months, provided there is no family history of allergy.

It is important to only buy packaged food that is labelled 'nut free'; loose bakery products, sweets and chocolates may contain nuts. Children under the age of five shouldn't be given whole nuts because of the risk of choking.

Gluten

Gluten is found in wheat, rye, barley and oats. Foods containing gluten, such as bread or pasta, should not be introduced into any baby's diet before six months.

When buying baby cereals and rusks, choose varieties that are gluten free. Baby rice is the safest to try at first, and thereafter there are plenty of alternative gluten-free products such as soya, corn, rice, millet rice noodles and buckwheat spaghetti, and potato flours for thickening and baking.

In some cases intolerance to wheat and similar proteins is temporary, and children may grow out of the condition before they are two or three years old. However, although it is rare, some people suffer from a permanent sensitivity to gluten known as coeliac disease. Symptoms include loss of appetite, poor growth, swollen abdomen and pale and particularly smelly stools. Coeliac disease can be diagnosed by a blood test and can be confirmed by looking at the gut wall using endoscopy.

PREPARING BABY FOODS

Preparing and cooking baby foods isn't difficult but, because you're dealing with a baby, considerations like hygiene must be of the utmost importance. Always wash fruit and vegetables carefully before cooking.

Equipment

Most of the equipment you require will already be in your kitchen – mashers, graters, sieves, etc. – but the following three pieces may not be, and I consider them to be vital!

Mouli   This hand-turned food mill with variable cutting discs purées the food, separating it from the seeds and tough fibres which can be difficult for the baby to digest. It is ideal for foods like dried apricots, sweetcorn or green beans.

Blender or food processor   This is useful for puréeing larger quantities. However, foods for young babies will often need to be sieved afterwards, before serving, in order to remove any indigestible seeds and skin.

Steamer   It is worth buying a multi-tiered steamer, so you can cook several foods at once. (A colander over a saucepan with a well-fitting lid is a cheaper alternative.)

Sterilising

At first, it is very important to sterilise bottles properly, and particularly the teats that your baby sucks, by whatever approved method you choose. Warm milk is the perfect breeding ground for bacteria and, if bottles are not properly washed and sterilised, your baby can become very ill. It would be impossible, however, to sterilise *all* the equipment you use for cooking and puréeing baby food, but take extra care to keep everything very clean.

Use a dishwasher if you have one; the water is at a much higher temperature than it would be possible to use if washing the utensils by hand, which helps to sterilise your equipment. However, once it is removed from the dishwasher, it does not remain sterile; bottles should be filled with milk immediately and stored in the fridge. Dry utensils with kitchen paper rather than a non-sterile tea towel.

All milk bottles should continue to be sterilised until your baby is one year old, but there is really not much point sterilising spoons or food containers beyond the age when your baby starts to crawl and put everything in reach into his mouth. There is no need to sterilise any other feeding equipment, but do wash bowls and spoons in a dishwasher or by hand at about 27°C/80°F – you will need to wear rubber gloves. If using a food mixer it is a good idea to rinse it out with boiling water as they are a common breeding ground for bugs.

Steaming

Steam the vegetables or fruits until tender. This is the best way to preserve the fresh taste and vitamins. Vitamins B and C are water soluble and can easily be destroyed by overcooking, especially when foods are boiled in water. Broccoli loses over 60 per cent of its antioxidants when boiled, but less than 7 per cent when steamed.

Boiling

Peel, seed or stone the vegetables or fruits as necessary and cut into pieces. Try to use the minimum amount of water and be careful not to overcook. To make a smooth purée, add just enough of the cooking liquid or a small amount of formula or breast milk.

Microwaving

Place the vegetables or fruit in a suitable dish. Add a little water, cover leaving an air vent and cook on full power until tender (stir halfway through). Purée to the desired consistency. Check that it isn't too hot to serve to your baby and stir well to avoid hot spots.

Baking

If you are cooking a meal for the family in the oven, you could use the opportunity to bake a potato, sweet potato or butternut squash for your baby. Prick the chosen vegetable with a fork and bake until tender. Cut in half, (remove the seeds from the squash) scoop out the flesh and mash together with some water or milk.

Freezing Baby Foods

Preparing tiny amounts of purée can be difficult. It is much better to prepare more than you need and freeze extra portions in ice-cube trays or small pots. You can then plan your baby's meals so that you only need to cook once or twice a week.

Cook and purée the food, cover and cool as quickly as possible. To preserve the quality of the food, it is very important that any foods that are to be frozen are well sealed to prevent the food drying out. It is also best if the container is filled almost to the top rather than leaving a large pocket of air above the food. It should be stored in a freezer that will freeze food to $-18°C/$ $0°F$ or below in 24 hours.

In the early stages of weaning, flexible plastic ice-cube trays are ideal for freezing baby food, but make sure you wrap them in polythene freezer bags. Once frozen,

knock the cubes out and store them in freezer bags, labelling them with the expiry date so you never give food that is past its best. Squeeze out as much air as possible before sealing securely, in order to maximise storage life. Once your baby starts eating larger portions it is a good idea to buy some small, plastic containers with snap-on lids that are designed for freezing baby food.

To thaw one meal, remove the relevant number of cubes from the bag (if there is time, leave the food to defrost before heating) and heat in a small pan or microwave until piping hot all the way through (stir thoroughly if heating in a microwave). Allow the food to cool down and always test the temperature before feeding your baby as their mouths are more sensitive to heat than ours. Fruit that is to be served cold can be defrosted in the fridge overnight. There are some rules regarding frozen food.

- Never refreeze meals that have already been frozen; however, if using frozen vegetables or fruit to make baby purées they can be cooked and refrozen.
- Never reheat meals more than once.
- Baby foods can be stored in a freezer for up to 8 weeks.

INTRODUCING PARTICULAR FOODS

I have listed below particular foods that you should avoid feeding your baby until a certain age has been reached. This is not an exhaustive list and you should refer to each chapter for more information.

WHEN CAN THEY HAVE ...?	
Gluten (wheat, rye, barley and oats)	*6 months*
Citrus fruits	*6 months*
Well-cooked eggs	*6–9 months*
Soft eggs, e.g. well-cooked scrambled eggs	*from 1 year*
Added salt	*limited amount from 12 months*
Sugar	*limited amount from 12 months*
Whole cow's milk as a main drink	*12 months*
Honey	*12 months*
Paté	*12 months*
Soft/blue cheese e.g. Brie/Gorgonzola	*12 months*
Whole/chopped nuts	*5 years*

MEAL PLANNERS

In the next chapter I've devised some meal planners to help you through the first weeks when you start to wean your baby. The First Tastes Meal Planner shows how to gradually wean your baby onto solids using mainly single ingredient, easily digested fruit and vegetable purées that are unlikely to provoke an allergic reaction. Once your baby has been introduced to these tastes, progress to the After First Tastes Accepted Meal Planner, which includes combinations of fruit and vegetable purées like carrot and pea or peaches, apples and pears. Adapt the recipes according to what is in season.

These planners are intended only as a guide and will depend on many factors including weight. If your baby's last meal is close to bedtime, avoid giving him anything that is heavy or difficult to digest. This is certainly not the time to experiment with new foods if you both want a good night's sleep.

I have tried to give a wide choice of recipes, although I expect that, in practice, meals that your baby enjoys would be repeated several times – and this is where your freezer will come in handy.

In each subsequent chapter, there are meal planners for your baby which you may follow or simply use as a guide. Adapt the charts according to what is in season and what you are preparing for your family. From nine months onwards, you should be able to cook for your baby and family together, perhaps eating the recipes

you give your baby for lunch and tea for your own supper, provided you do not add salt to your baby's portion.

In these later charts, I have set out four meals a day, but many babies are satisfied with just three meals as well as some healthy snacks.

Many of the vegetable purées in the early chapters can be transformed into a vegetable soup; and a number of the vegetable dishes can serve as good side dishes for the family. Again, if you give the baby some of the vegetables you are preparing for the family, make sure they have not been salted. In the later chapters many recipes are suitable for the whole family.

After each recipe is a symbol of two faces – one smiling ☺, the other gloomy ☹ – each with a tick box. You will find these useful for recording your successes (or otherwise)! Some recipes also show a snowflake ❄, which means the meal is suitable for freezing.

CHAPTER TWO

FIRST-STAGE WEANING

In the recent past there was a lot of pressure on parents to start their babies on solids too early – this pressure was variously commercial, medical and social (keeping up with the Jones's baby!). Ideas have now changed, and this is all to the good, for many ordinary foods, as already discussed, can cause allergies. Neither is a baby's digestive system capable of absorbing foods more complex than baby milk until the age of at least seventeen weeks.

The UK Department of Health guidelines recommend breastfeeding exclusively for the first six months as that should meet all your baby's nutritional needs. If a baby is being given formula milk she will need 600–800 ml/21–28 fl oz a day between four and six months, and 500–800 ml/18–28 fl oz a day between six months and one year once she starts on solids.

FIRST FRUITS AND VEGETABLES

Very first foods should be easy to digest and unlikely to provoke an allergic reaction.

I find that root vegetables like carrot, sweet potato, parsnip and swede tend to be the most popular with very young babies due to their naturally sweet flavour and smooth texture once puréed. The best first fruits for young babies are apple, pear, banana and papaya, but it's important that you choose fruit that is ripe and has a good flavour, so it's a good idea to taste it yourself before giving it to your baby.

Until recently, the advice given was to introduce each food separately, waiting for three days before introducing another new food. However, unless there is a history of allergy or you are concerned about your baby's reactions to a certain food, there is no reason why new foods should not be introduced on consecutive days, provided you keep to the list in the table.

Take care when introducing solids *not to reduce your baby's milk intake*, as milk is still the most important factor in growth and development.

It is important to wean your baby on as wide a range of foods as possible. After first tastes are accepted you can introduce all fruit and vegetables (see page 27). However, take care with citrus, pineapple, berry fruits and kiwi fruit as these may upset some susceptible babies.

Fruit

At first a baby should have cooked purées of fruits like apples and pears, or uncooked mashed banana or papaya. After the first few weeks your baby can graduate to other raw mashed or puréed fruits like melon, peach and plum – these are delicious as long as they are ripe.

Dried fruits can be introduced but in small quantities; although they are nutritious they tend to be laxatives. If you are worried about the use of pesticides, organic fruit and vegetables are available.

Vegetables

Some people prefer to start their babies on vegetables rather than fruit. Because

---

BEST FIRST FRUITS

Apple
Pear
Banana*
Papaya*

BEST FIRST VEGETABLES

Carrot
Potato
Swede
Parsnip
Pumpkin
Butternut squash
Sweet potato

* Banana and papaya do not require cooking provided they are ripe. They can be puréed or mashed on their own or together with a little breast or formula milk. Bananas are not suitable for freezing.

most babies will take to eating fruit quite happily, they feel it is important to establish a liking for more savoury tastes.

At the beginning, when introducing a baby to solids, it is best to start with root vegetables, particularly carrots, since they are naturally sweet. Different vegetables provide different vitamins and minerals (for instance, green vegetables provide Vitamin C, and yellow provide Vitamin A) so a variety is of value at later stages.

Many vegetables have quite strong flavours – broccoli, for example – so when solids are fairly well established, you could mix in some potato or baby rice and milk to make it more palatable. Very young babies like their food quite bland.

Note that all fruit and vegetables can also be cooked in a microwave (see page 17 for general method).

Rice

Another good first food is baby rice. Mixed with water or breast or formula milk, it is easily digested and its milky taste makes for a smooth transition to solids. Choose one that is sugar free and enriched with vitamins and iron. Baby rice also combines well with both fruit and vegetable purées.

TEXTURES

At the very beginning of weaning, the rice and fruit or vegetable purées should be fairly wet and soft. This means that most vegetables, for instance, should be cooked until very soft so that they purée easily. You will probably need to thin out the consistency of the purées, since babies are more likely to accept food in a semi-liquid form. You can use formula or breast milk, fruit juice or boiled water.

As your baby becomes more accustomed to the feel of 'solid food' in her mouth, you can gradually start to reduce the amount of liquid that you are adding to the purées, which will encourage her to chew a little. This should be a natural process as she should want to chew her food as she starts teething (usually between six and twelve months). You could also *thicken* the purées if necessary with baby rice or some crumbled rusk. As the baby becomes older and solid feeding is established (at the age of about six months), some fruit can be served raw and vegetables can be cooked more lightly (retaining more Vitamin C). Food can also be mashed or finely chopped to encourage chewing later on.

Remember to peel, core and deseed fruits as necessary before cooking and/or puréeing (or put them through a mouli). Vegetables with fibres or seeds should be sieved or put through a mouli for a smooth texture. The husks of leguminous vegetables cannot be digested at this stage.

QUANTITIES

At the very beginning, don't expect your baby to take more than 1–2 teaspoons of her baby rice or a fruit or vegetable purée. For this you should need one portion – in this section, this means one or two cubes from an ice-cube tray.

As your baby gets used to eating solids you may need to defrost three or more frozen food-cubes for her meal, or start freezing food in larger pots.

DRINKS

Water, as outlined on page 13, is the best drink to offer. But freshly squeezed orange juice is high in Vitamin C, which helps your child to absorb iron. If your baby reacts to orange juice you can offer blackcurrant or rosehip instead. Dilute one part juice to at least five parts cooled boiled water. Diluted juice tastes weak to us but babies don't miss the sweet taste as they haven't been used to it. Try to avoid giving sweet drinks as this will give them a sweet tooth and result in them no longer accepting water.

If you buy commercial fruit juices, they should be unsweetened. But even those labelled 'unsweetened' or 'no added sugar' still contain sugars and acids that can lead to tooth decay. It is important not to let your baby continually sip any fluid except water.

A juicer is a useful machine to have in the kitchen when there is a baby in the house. Many fruits *and* vegetables can be turned into nutritious drinks.

TIPS FOR INTRODUCING SOLIDS

1 Make the rice or purée fairly wet and soft at first, using breast or formula milk, an unsweetened juice or cooking water. A handy tip is to mix the purée in the plastic removable top of a feeding bottle (which has been sterilised).

2 Hold your baby comfortably on your lap or sit her in her baby chair. It would be better if *both* of you were protected against spills!

3 Choose a time when your baby is not frantically hungry and maybe give her some milk first to partially satisfy her – she will then be more receptive to the new idea.

4 Babies are unable to lick food off a spoon with their tongues, so choose a small, *shallow* plastic teaspoon off which she can take some food with her lips. (Special weaning spoons can be bought.)

5 Start by giving just one solid feed during the day, about 1–2 tea spoons to begin with. I prefer to give this feed at lunch-time.

FRUIT AND VEGETABLES

FIRST TASTES

Apple

Choose a sweet variety of eating apple. Peel, halve, core and chop 2 medium apples. Put into a heavy saucepan with 4–5 tablespoons water. Cover and cook over a low heat until tender (7–8 minutes). Or steam for the same length of time. Purée. If steaming, add some of the boiled water from the bottom of the steamer to thin out the purée.

Apple and Cinnamon

Simmer 2 apples in apple juice or water with a cinnamon stick. Cook as above; remove stick before puréeing.

MAKES 5 PORTIONS

Pear

Peel, halve and core 2 pears, then cut into small pieces. Cover with a little water, cook over a low heat until soft (about 4 minutes). Or steam for the same length of time. Purée. After the first few weeks of weaning, you can purée ripe pears without cooking. Apple and pear together makes a good combination.

MAKES 5 PORTIONS

Banana

Mashed banana makes ideal baby food. It is easy to digest and rarely causes allergic reactions. Choose a ripe banana and mash very well with a fork to make it as smooth as possible. Add a little boiled water or baby milk if it is too thick and sticky for your baby to swallow.

If your baby is suffering from diarrhoea or a stomach upset, a diet of mashed banana, cooked apple purée and baby rice for a few days is a good remedy.

MAKES 1 PORTION

Papaya

Papaya is an excellent fruit to give a very young baby. It has a pleasing sweet taste which is not too strong and blends within seconds to a perfect texture.

Cut a medium fruit in half, remove all the black seeds and scoop out the flesh. Purée, adding a little formula or breast milk if you like.

MAKES 4 PORTIONS

Cream of Fruit

Combining a fruit purée with baby milk and baby rice or crumbled rusk can make it more palatable for your baby. In the next few months, when your baby may start eating some other exotic fruits like mango and kiwi fruit, this method of 'diluting' the fruit purée with milk will also make them less acidic.

Peel, core, steam or boil and purée the fruit as described and, for each 1 portion quantity of pre-pared fruit, stir in 1 tablespoon unflavoured baby rice or half a low-sugar rusk and 2 tablespoons baby milk.

MAKES 3 EXTRA PORTIONS

Three-Fruit Purée

This is a delicious combination of three of the first fruits that your baby can eat.

Mix 1 dessertspoon each of pear and apple purées (see page 24) with half a banana, mashed. You could also use half a raw ripe pear, peeled, cored and cut into chunks. Purée this and the half banana in a blender until smooth, then mix together with the dessert-spoon of cooked apple purée.

MAKES 4 PORTIONS

Carrot or Parsnip

Peel, trim and slice 2 medium carrots or parsnips. Place in a saucepan of lightly boiling water, cover and simmer for 25 minutes or until very tender. Alternatively, you can steam them. Drain, reserving the cooking liquid and purée to a smooth consistency, adding as much of the reserved liquid as necessary.

The cooking time is longer for small babies. Once your baby can chew, cut the cooking time down to preserve Vitamin C and keep the vegetables crisper.

MAKES 4 PORTIONS

Sweet Potato, Swede or Parsnip

Use a large sweet potato, a small swede or two large parsnips. Scrub, peel and chop into small cubes. Cover with boiling water and simmer, covered, until tender (15–20 minutes). Alternatively, steam the vegetables. Drain, reserving the cooking liquid. Purée in a blender adding some liquid if necessary.

MAKES 4 PORTIONS

Potato

Wash, peel and chop 400 g/14 oz potatoes, just cover with boiling water and cook over a medium heat for about 15 minutes. Blend with some cooking liquid or baby milk to make the desired consistency. Alternatively, steam the potatoes and blend with some water from the steamer or your baby's usual milk.

Avoid using a food processor to purée potato as it breaks down the starch and makes a sticky pulp. Use a mouli instead.

You can bake potato or sweet potato in the oven. Preheat to 200°C /400°F/Gas 6 for 1–1¼ hours or until soft. Scoop out the inside and mouli or mash with a little baby milk and a knob of butter.

MAKES 10 PORTIONS

Cream of Carrot

A creamy purée can be made with many different vegetables by adding milk and baby rice. Make a purée with one large carrot (approx. 85 g/3 oz). This should make about 100 ml/3½ fl oz carrot purée (see page 25). Mix 1 tablespoon unflavoured baby rice with 2 tablespoons of your baby's usual milk. Stir the baby rice mixture into the vegetable purée. Half a low-sugar rusk crushed and mixed with milk will also make a creamy purée. Allow the rusk to soften in the baby milk before mixing it into the vegetable purée of your choice.

MAKES 2 PORTIONS

Butternut Squash

Butternut squash has a naturally sweet flavour that is very popular with babies.

Peel a butternut squash weighing about 350 g/12 oz. Deseed and cut the flesh into 2½ cm/ 1 inch cubes. Steam or cover with boiling water and simmer for about 15 minutes or until tender. Transfer the squash to a blender and make a purée with a little of the cooking liquid.

MAKES 6 PORTIONS

FRUIT AND VEGETABLES
AFTER FIRST TASTES ACCEPTED

Courgette

Wash 2 medium courgettes carefully, remove the ends and slice. (The skin is soft so doesn't need to be removed.) Steam until tender (about 10 minutes), then purée in a blender or mash with a fork. (No need to add extra liquid.) Good mixed with sweet potato, carrot or baby rice.

MAKES 8 PORTIONS

Broccoli and Cauliflower

Use 100 g/4 oz of either. Wash well, cut into small florets and add 150 ml/5 fl oz boiling water. Simmer, covered, until tender (about 10 minutes). Drain, reserving the cooking liquid. Purée until smooth, adding a little of the liquid, or baby milk, to make the desired consistency.

Alternatively, steam the florets for 10 minutes for better flavour and retention of nutrients. Add water from the steamer, or baby milk, to make a smooth purée. Broccoli and cauliflower are good mixed with a cheese sauce or root vegetable purée like carrot or sweet potato.

MAKES 4 PORTIONS

Green Beans

French beans are best since they tend to be the least stringy variety; runner beans should be puréed in a mouli. Wash the beans, top and tail, and remove any stringy bits. Steam until tender (about 12 minutes), then blend. Add a little boiled water or baby milk to make a smooth purée. Green vegetables like beans are good mixed with root vegetables such as sweet potato or carrot.

Potato, Courgette and Broccoli

Combining potato with green vegetables makes them more palatable for babies. Peel and chop two medium potatoes (200 g/7 oz). Boil in water below a steamer for about 10 minutes or until soft. Place 25 g/1 oz broccoli florets and 50 g/2 oz sliced courgette in the steamer basket, cover and cook for 5 minutes or until all the vegetables are tender. Drain the potato and purée all the vegetables in a mouli, adding enough baby milk to make a smooth consistency.

MAKES 4 PORTIONS

Broccoli Trio

Peel and chop a medium sweet potato (approx. 200 g/7 oz) and boil for 5 minutes. Place 50 g/2 oz each of broccoli and cauliflower florets in a steamer basket above the sweet potato, cover and continue to cook for 5 minutes. When all the vegetables are tender, purée them in a blender together with a knob of butter and enough of the cooking liquid to make the desired consistency.

MAKES 4 PORTIONS

Carrot and Cauliflower

Combining vegetables makes them more interesting and, once your baby has got used to carrot and cauliflower separately, this combination makes a nice change. Cook 50 g/2 oz carrots, scraped and sliced, in boiling water for 20 minutes until soft. After 10 minutes, add 175 g/6 oz cauliflower florets. Drain the vegetables and purée in a blender. Stir in 2 tablespoons baby milk.

MAKES 4 PORTIONS

Peach

Bring a small saucepan of water to the boil. Cut a shallow cross on the skin of 2 peaches, submerge them in the water for 1 minute, then plunge into cold water. Skin and chop the peaches, discarding the stones. Either purée the peaches uncooked or steam first for a few minutes until tender. Peach and banana makes a good combination.

MAKES 4 PORTIONS

Cantaloupe Melon

Cantaloupes are the small, very pale green melons with orange flesh. They are rich in Vitamins A and C. Only give ripe melon. Cut in half, remove seeds, scoop out the flesh and purée in a blender.

Other varieties of sweet melon like Galia or Honeydew are good too. When your baby is a little older, properly ripe melon may be eaten raw.

MAKES 6 PORTIONS

Plum

Skin 2 large ripe plums as for peaches (see opposite). Purée in a blender – the fruit can be puréed uncooked if soft and juicy or you could steam the plums for a few minutes until tender. Plums are good mixed with baby rice, banana or yoghurt.

MAKES 4 PORTIONS

Dried Apricot, Peach or Prune

Many supermarkets stock a selection of ready-to-eat dried fruits. Dried apricots are particularly nutritious, being rich in beta-carotene and iron. Cover 100 g/4 oz fruit with fresh cold water, bring to the boil and simmer until soft (about 5 minutes). Drain, remove the stones and press through a mouli to remove the rough skins. Add a little of the cooking liquid to make a smooth purée.

This is good combined with baby rice and milk, banana or ripe pear.

MAKES 4 PORTIONS

Apricot and Pear

Roughly chop 50 g/2 oz ready-to-eat dried apricots and put them into a saucepan with 2 ripe Conference pears (350 g/12 oz) peeled, cored and cut into pieces. Cook, covered, over a low heat for 3–4 minutes. Purée in a blender. Alternatively, use 4 fresh, sweet, ripe apricots, peeled, stoned and chopped.

MAKES 8 PORTIONS

Apple and Raisin Compote

Heat 3 tablespoons of fresh orange juice in a saucepan. Add 2 eating apples peeled, cored and sliced, and 15 g/½ oz of washed raisins. Cook gently for about 5 minutes until soft, adding a little water if necessary.

Dried fruit like apricots or raisins should be put through a mouli for young babies, to get rid of the outer skin which is difficult to digest.

MAKES 8 PORTIONS

Peas

I tend to use frozen peas as they are just as nutritious as fresh. Cover 100 g/4 oz peas with water, bring to the boil and simmer, covered, for 4 minutes until tender. Drain, reserving some cooking liquid. Purée using a mouli or press through a sieve and add some of the cooking liquid to make the desired consistency. Good combined with potato, sweet potato, parsnip or carrot. If using fresh peas, cook them for 12–15 minutes.

MAKES 4 PORTIONS

Sweet Red Pepper

Wash, core and deseed a medium pepper. Cut into quarters and roast under a pre-heated grill until the skin is charred. Place in a plastic bag and allow to cool. Peel off the blistered skin and purée. Good with cauliflower or potato.

MAKES 2–3 PORTIONS

Avocado

Cut a well-ripened avocado in half and scoop out the stone. Use $^1/_3$–$^1/_2$ and mash the flesh with a fork, maybe adding a little milk. Serve quickly to avoid it turning brown. Good mixed with mashed banana. Do not freeze avocados.

MAKES 1 PORTION

Corn on the Cob

Remove the outer corn husks and silk from the corn on the cob and rinse well. Cover with boiling water and cook over a medium heat for 10 minutes. Strain and then remove the kernels of corn using a sharp knife. Purée in a mouli. Alternatively, cook some frozen corn and then purée.

MAKES 2 PORTIONS

Spinach

Wash 100 g/4 oz spinach leaves very carefully, removing the coarse stalks. Either steam the spinach or put in a saucepan and sprinkle with a little water. Cook until the leaves are wilted (about 3–4 minutes). Gently press out any excess water. Good combined with potato, sweet potato or butternut squash.

MAKES 2 PORTIONS

Tomatoes

Plunge 2 medium tomatoes in boiling water for 30 seconds. Transfer to cold water, skin, seed and roughly chop. Melt a knob of butter in a heavy-bottomed saucepan and sauté the tomato until mushy. Purée in a blender. This is good combined with potato, cauliflower or courgette.

MAKES 2–3 PORTIONS

Peach and Banana

This is a delicious purée to make when peaches are in season. They are a good source of Vitamin C and are easy to digest. Banana also combines well with papaya.

MAKES 1 PORTION

1 ripe peach, skinned and cut into pieces   *½ tablespoon pure apple juice*
1 small banana, peeled and sliced   *baby rice (optional)*

Put the peach, banana and apple juice into a small pan, cover and simmer for 2 3 minutes. Purée in a blender. If it's too runny, add a little baby rice.

Apple and Banana with Orange Juice

This makes a nice change from plain mashed banana or apple purée. When your baby is six months or older, you can make this with raw grated apple and mashed banana.

MAKES 1 PORTION

¼ apple, peeled, cored and chopped   *1 teaspoon orange juice*
¼ banana, peeled and chopped

Steam the apple until tender (about 7 minutes), then purée or smash it together with the banana and orange juice. Serve as soon as possible.

Peaches, Apples and Pears

When peaches aren't in season you can make this just using apples and pears. If the purée is too thin, stir in some baby rice to thicken it.

MAKES 8 PORTIONS

2 eating apples, peeled, cored and chopped
1 vanilla pod

2 tablespoons apple juice or water
2 ripe peaches, skinned and chopped
2 ripe pears, peeled, cored and chopped

Put the chopped apple in a saucepan. Split the vanilla pod with a sharp knife, scrape the seeds into the pan and add the pod and 2 tablespoons apple juice or water. Simmer, covered, for about 5 minutes. Add the peaches and pears and cook for 3–4 minutes more. Remove the pod and purée.

Mixed Dried-Fruit Compote

Dried fruits and fresh fruits are delicious combined. You can buy packets of mixed ready-to-eat dried fruit in most supermarkets.

MAKES 6 PORTIONS

50 g/2 oz each dried apricots, dried peaches and prunes

1 eating apple and 1 pear, peeled, cored and chopped, or 1 apple and 3 fresh apricots, skinned, stoned and chopped

Put the dried fruit, apple and pear (or apricot, if using) into a saucepan and just cover with boiling water. Simmer for about 8 minutes. Drain the fruit and purée, adding a little of the cooking liquid if necessary.

Vegetable Stock

Vegetable stock forms the basis of many vegetable recipes. This should keep for a week in the fridge and it is well worth making your own, which will be free from additives and salt.

MAKES ABOUT 900 ML/1½ PINTS

1 large onion, peeled
125 g/4½ oz carrot, peeled
1 celery stalk
175 g/6 oz mixed root vegetables (sweet potato, swede, parsnip), peeled
½ leek

25 g/1 oz butter
1 sachet bouquet garni
1 sprig of fresh parsley and 1 bay leaf
6 black peppercorns
900 ml/1½ pints water

Chop all the vegetables. Melt the butter in a large saucepan and sauté the onion for 5 minutes. Add the remaining ingredients and cover with the water. Bring to the boil and simmer for about 1 hour. Strain the stock and squeeze any remaining juices from the vegetables through a sieve.

Carrot and Pea Purée

Both carrots and peas have a naturally sweet taste that appeals to babies.

MAKES 2 PORTIONS

200 g/7 oz carrots, peeled and sliced

40 g/1½ oz frozen peas

Put the sliced carrots in a saucepan and cover with boiling water. Cook, covered, for 15 minutes. Add the peas and cook for a further 5 minutes. Purée with sufficient cooking liquid to make a smooth purée.

Baby Cereal and Vegetables

Sometimes vegetable purées can be very watery – particularly those made from, say, courgettes, which have a high water content. In this recipe I have added baby rice, which makes an excellent thickening agent.

MAKES 6 PORTIONS

25 g/1 oz onion, peeled and chopped
1 teaspoon olive oil
1 medium courgette, trimmed and sliced
50 g/2 oz broccoli

2 medium carrots, peeled and sliced
vegetable stock (optional)
50 g/2 oz frozen peas
3 tablespoons baby rice

Sauté the onion in the olive oil for 2 minutes, then add all the vegetables except the frozen peas. Just cover with boiling water or vegetable stock. Bring back to the boil, then simmer for 20 minutes. Add the frozen peas and cook for 5 minutes more. Purée the vegetables, adding as much of the cooking liquid as necessary to make the desired consistency, and stir in the baby rice.

Sweet Vegetable Medley

Root vegetables like swede, carrot and parsnip make delicious and nutritious purées for young babies. Butternut squash and pumpkin can also be used to make this purée as, again, they are very popular with babies.

MAKES 5 PORTIONS

100 g/4 oz carrot, peeled and chopped
100 g/4 oz swede, peeled and chopped
100 g/4 oz potato, butternut squash or pumpkin, peeled and chopped

50 g/2 oz parsnip, peeled and chopped
300 ml/10 fl oz water or milk (can use cow's milk in cooking from six months)

Put the vegetables in a saucepan with the water or milk. Bring to the boil, then cover and simmer for 25–30 minutes or until the vegetables are tender. Remove with a slotted spoon and purée the vegetables in a blender, together with as much cooking liquid as necessary to make the desired consistency.

Watercress, Potato and Courgette Purée

Watercress is rich in calcium and iron. It blends well with the other vegetables to make a tasty, bright green purée. You can add a little milk if your baby prefers it that way.

MAKES 6 PORTIONS

1 large potato (approx. 300 g / 11 oz), peeled and chopped
300 ml / 10 fl oz vegetable stock (see page 33)

1 medium courgette (approx. 100 g / 4 oz), trimmed and sliced
a small bunch of watercress
a little milk (optional)

Put the potato into a saucepan, cover with the stock and cook for 5 minutes. Add the sliced courgette and continue to cook for another 5 minutes. Trim the stalks of the watercress, add to the potato and cook for 2–3 minutes. Purée the mixture in a mouli and, if you like, add a little milk to adjust the consistency.

Avocado and Banana or Papaya

This is very simple to make and the fruits blend very well.

MAKES 1 PORTION

½ small avocado   *½ small banana or ¼ papaya*

Remove the flesh from the avocado and mash with the banana or papaya until smooth. This should be eaten soon after it is made or the avocado will turn brown.

Butternut Squash and Pear

Butternut squash is one of the more unusual vegetables now available in supermarkets. It is easily digested, rarely causes allergies, and is a good source of Vitamin A. Babies like its naturally sweet taste, which combines well with fruit; and cooking fruit and vegetables in a steamer, as here, is one of the best ways of preserving nutrients. Butternut squash is also delicious if you cut it in half, scoop out the seeds, brush each half with melted butter, and spoon 1 tablespoon of fresh orange juice into each cavity. Cover with foil and bake in the oven at 180°C/350°F/Gas 4 for 1½ hours or until tender.

MAKES 4 PORTIONS

1 medium butternut squash or pumpkin   *1 ripe juicy pear*
    (about 450 g/1 lb)

Peel the butternut squash, cut in half, remove the seeds and chop into pieces. Steam for about 12 minutes. Peel, core and chop the pear, add to the steamer and continue to cook for 5 minutes or until the squash is tender. Purée in a blender.

Sweet Potato with Cinnamon

The addition of cinnamon gives this an extra sweetness, which babies love. This is very simple to make.

MAKES 4 PORTIONS

1 sweet potato (about 175 g/6 oz), peeled and cut into chunks

a generous pinch of ground cinnamon a few tablespoons baby milk

Cover the sweet potato chunks with water, bring to the boil and simmer for about 30 minutes or until soft. Drain and mash together with the cinnamon and enough baby milk to make the desired consistency.

Leek, Sweet Potato and Pea Purée

Sweet potatoes make perfect baby food; they are full of nutrients and have a naturally sweet taste and smooth texture. Choose the orange-fleshed variety as it is rich in betacarotene. It is fine to use frozen vegetables in baby purées as they are frozen within hours of being picked and can be just as nutritious as fresh vegetables. Once cooked, frozen vegetables can be refrozen.

MAKES 5 PORTIONS

50 g/2 oz leek, washed and sliced 400 g/14 oz sweet potato, peeled and chopped

300 ml/10 fl oz vegetable stock 50 g/2 oz frozen peas

Put the leek and chopped sweet potato in a saucepan, pour over the vegetable stock and bring to the boil. Cover and simmer for 15 minutes. Add the peas and continue to cook for 5 minutes. Purée in a blender.

FIRST TASTES MEAL PLANNER

Week 1	Early morning	Breakfast	Lunch	Tea	Bedtime
Days 1–2	Breast/bottle	Breast/bottle	Breast/bottle, Baby rice	Breast/bottle	Breast/bottle
Days 3–4	Breast/bottle	Breast/bottle	Breast/bottle Root Vegetable e.g. carrot or sweet potato	Breast/bottle	Breast/bottle
Day 5	Breast/bottle	Breast/bottle	Breast/bottle Pear with baby rice	Breast/bottle	Breast/bottle
Day 6	Breast/bottle	Breast/bottle	Breast/bottle Apple	Breast/bottle	Breast/bottle
Day 7	Breast/bottle	Breast/bottle	Breast/bottle Vegetable e.g. butternut squash or sweet potato	Breast/bottle	Breast/bottle
Week 2					
Days 1–2	Breast/bottle Apple or pear with baby rice	Breast/bottle	Breast/bottle Root Vegetable e.g. potato, parsnip or carrot	Breast/bottle	Breast/bottle
Days 3–4	Breast/bottle Banana or papaya	Breast/bottle	Breast/bottle **Sweet Vegetable Medley**	Breast/bottle	Breast/bottle
Days 5–6	Breast/bottle Apple or pear	Breast/bottle	Breast/bottle Sweet potato, butternut squash or swede	Breast/bottle	Breast/bottle
Day 7	Breast/bottle Peach and banana or mashed banana	Breast/bottle	Breast/bottle Carrot or carrot and parsnip	Breast/bottle	Breast/bottle

These charts are intended only as a guide and will depend on many factors including weight. Some babies may only want one solid feed a day and some may prefer to have a second meal at tea-time. Bold type indicates recipes shown in the book.

FIRST TASTES MEAL PLANNER

Week 3	Early morning	Breakfast	Lunch	Tea	Bedtime
Day 1	Breast/bottle	Breast/bottle Banana	Diluted juice or water **Sweet Vegetable Medley**	Breast/bottle	Breast/bottle
Day 2	Breast/bottle	Breast/bottle Apple	Diluted juice or water **Sweet Vegetable Medley**	Breast/bottle	Breast/bottle
Day 3	Breast/bottle	Breast/bottle **Peaches, Apples and Pears**	Diluted juice or water **Broccoli Trio**	Breast/bottle	Breast/bottle
Day 4	Breast/bottle	Breast/bottle **Cream of Fruit**	Diluted juice or water **Butternut Squash and Pear**	Breast/bottle	Breast/bottle
Day 5	Breast/bottle	Breast/bottle **Cream of Fruit**	Diluted juice or water **Butternut Squash and Pear**	Breast/bottle	Breast/bottle
Day 6	Breast/bottle	Breast/bottle Banana or papaya	Diluted juice or water **Potato, Courgette and Broccoli**	Breast/bottle	Breast/bottle
Day 7	Breast/bottle	Breast/bottle Pear or baby rice	Diluted juice or water **Carrot and Pea Purée**	Breast/bottle	Breast/bottle

Fruit juice should be diluted at least three parts water to one part juice, or substituted completely, with cooled boiled water.

AFTER FIRST TASTES ACCEPTED MEAL PLANNER

	Early morning	*Breakfast*	*Lunch*	*Tea*	*Bedtime*
Day 1	Breast/bottle	Breast/bottle **Three-Fruit Purée**	**Leek, Sweet Potato and Pea Purée** Breast/bottle	**Carrot and Cauliflower** Water or diluted juice	Breast/bottle
Day 2	Breast/bottle	Breast/bottle **Three-Fruit Purée**	**Leek, Sweet Potato and Pea Purée** Breast/bottle	**Sweet Vegetable Medley** Water or diluted juice	Breast/bottle
Day 3	Breast/bottle	Breast/bottle Pear and baby cereal	**Broccoli Trio** Breast/bottle	Sweet potato Water or diluted juice	Breast/bottle
Day 4	Breast/bottle	Breast/bottle **Apple and Cinnamon**	**Baby Cereal and Vegetables** Breast/bottle	Sweet potato Water or diluted juice	Breast/bottle
Day 5	Breast/bottle	Breast/bottle **Apple and Cinnamon** and baby cereal	**Avocado and Banana** Breast/bottle	**Carrot and Pea Purée** Water or diluted juice	Breast/bottle
Day 6	Breast/bottle	Breast/bottle Banana	**Watercress, Potato and Courgette Purée** Breast/bottle	**Broccoli Trio** Water or diluted juice	Breast/bottle
Day 7	Breast/bottle	Breast/bottle **Apple and Banana with Orange Juice**	**Watercress, Potato and Courgette Purée** Breast/bottle	**Broccoli Trio** Water or diluted juice	Breast/bottle

These charts are intended only as a guide and will depend on many factors including weight. Some babies will manage to eat some fruit after lunch and tea.

AFTER FIRST TASTES ACCEPTED MEAL PLANNER

	Breakfast	Mid-morning	Lunch	Mid-afternoon	Tea	Bedtime
Day 1	Breast/bottle Baby cereal Mashed banana	Breast/bottle	**Leek, Sweet Potato and Pea Purée** Water or diluted juice	Breast/bottle	Carrot Pear or Peach Rusk Water or diluted juice	Breast/bottle
Day 2	Breast/bottle Baby cereal **Apple and Raisin Compote**	Breast/bottle	**Avocado and Banana** Water or diluted juice	Breast/bottle	**Carrot and Pea Purée** Finely chopped melon or plum Water or diluted juice	Breast/bottle
Day 3	Breast/bottle Baby cereal **Apple and Banana with Orange Juice**	Breast/bottle	**Sweet Potato with Cinnamon** Water or diluted juice	Breast/bottle	**Potato, Courgette and Broccoli Mixed Dried-Fruit Compote** Water or diluted juice	Breast/bottle
Day 4	Breast/bottle Baby cereal Fromage frais	Breast/bottle	**Broccoli Trio** Water or diluted juice	Breast/bottle	**Sweet Vegetable Medley** Mango or papaya Water or diluted juice	Breast/bottle
Day 5	Breast/bottle Baby cereal **Peaches, Apples and Pears**	Breast/bottle	**Broccoli Trio** Water or diluted juice	Breast/bottle	**Sweet Vegetable Medley** Fingers of toast Yoghurt Water or diluted juice	Breast/bottle
Day 6	Breast/bottle Baby cereal **Peaches, Apples and Pears**	Breast/bottle	**Watercress, Potato and Courgette Purée** Water or diluted juice	Breast/bottle	**Leek, Sweet Potato and Pea Purée** Banana Water or diluted juice	Breast/bottle
Day 7	Breast/bottle Baby cereal **Apricot and Pear**	Breast/bottle	**Carrot and Pea Purée** Water or diluted juice	Breast/bottle	**Watercress, Potato and Courgette Purée Peach and Banana** Water or diluted juice	Breast/bottle

Fruit juice should be diluted at least three parts water to one part juice, or substituted completely, with cooled boiled water.

CHAPTER THREE

SECOND-STAGE
WEANING

Between seven and nine months is a rapid development period for your baby. A seven-month-old baby still needs to be supported whilst you are feeding him and, more often than not, still has no teeth. A nine-month-old baby, however, is usually strong enough to sit in a high chair whilst he is being fed and has already cut a few teeth. Babies of eight months are usually quite good at holding food themselves and enjoy eating small finger foods like pasta, pieces of raw or cooked vegetables or raw fruits. (Turn to pages 75–78 for suitable finger foods for young babies.) Babies are born with a store of iron that lasts for about six months. After this they rely on their diet for the iron they need. If a baby doesn't have at least 500 ml/18 fl oz breast milk or infant formula per day, his daily intake of iron is likely to be below the recommended level, and this can impair his mental and physical development. It is particularly important not to use ordinary cow's milk for your baby's regular drink before the age of one year as it doesn't contain as much iron or vitamins as formula milk.

LESS MILK, MORE APPETITE

Once your baby is seven to eight months old, you can start cutting down on his milk feeds so that he is more hungry for his solids. However, between six months and one year, babies should have 500–800 ml/18–28 fl oz breast milk or infant formula per day. In addition, you can give other dairy products, and offer water, diluted fruit juice or low-sugar herbal drinks with meals if your baby seems thirsty.

It is best to only put formula, breast milk or water into your baby's bottle. Comfort-sucking on sweetened drinks is the main cause of tooth decay in young children, and babies are more vulnerable to decay than children or adults. You should start using a lidded cup with a soft spout and easy-to-hold handles once your baby is six months old. There are training cups available to guide your baby from a soft spout to open drinking cup in easy stages.

Let your baby's appetite determine how much he eats and never force him to eat something he actually dislikes. Don't offer it for a while, but reintroduce it a few weeks later. You may find that second time around he loves it.

Remember, at this age it is normal for babies to be quite chubby. As soon as your baby starts crawling and walking, he will lose this excess weight.

THE FOODS TO CHOOSE

Your baby can now eat protein foods like eggs, cheese, pulses, chicken and fish. Limit some foods which might be indigestible – such as spinach, lentils, cheese, berry or citrus fruit – and don't worry if some foods, like pulses, peas and raisins, pass through your child undigested: until they are about two years old, babies cannot completely digest husked vegetables and the skins of fruits. Peeling, mashing and puréeing fruit and vegetables will of course aid digestion. With foods like bread, flour, pasta and rice, try to choose wholegrain, rather than refined, as it is more nutritious.

Once your baby has passed the six-month stage and is happily eating bread and other foods containing gluten, there is no longer any need to give him special baby cereals. You can use adult cereals like Ready Brek, instant porridge and Weetabix, which are just as nutritious and much cheaper. Choose a cereal that isn't highly refined and which is low in sugar and salt. Many people continue to use commercial baby foods because they think, due to the long list of vitamins and minerals on the packet, that they are more nutritious. However, babies who eat a good balanced diet of fresh foods get a perfectly adequate quantity of vitamins and minerals. Also, baby foods in general are heavily processed, and their finer texture and bland flavours will hinder the development of your baby's tastes.

Beware, too, of some of the rusks you can buy which are supposedly the 'ideal food for your baby'. They are full of sugar (some contain more sugar than a doughnut). Give your baby some toast to chew on or follow the simple recipe for rusks in the nine-to-twelve-month finger-food section (see page 76).

Ordinary cow's milk isn't suitable as your baby's main drink for the first year, as it doesn't contain enough iron or other nutrients for proper growth. However, whole cow's milk can be used in cooking or with cereal.

Fruit

Your baby should now be able to eat all fruits, and both fresh and dried fruits make a great snack. Different fruits contain different vitamins, so include as much variety as possible. Dried fruits are also a good source of other nutrients and energy. Take care to remove any stones before giving fruit, and don't give whole grapes to young babies as they may choke on them.

Vitamin C boosts iron absorption so it's important to include Vitamin C-rich fruits like citrus or berry fruits in your child's diet. It's good to give cereal with diluted orange juice in the morning. It also combines well with savoury foods like carrot, fish and liver.

To begin with, give berry and citrus fruits in small quantities as they can be indigestible, and some babies can have an adverse reaction to them. Combine them with other fruits like apple, banana, pear or peach. Kiwi fruit can also cause an allergic reaction in some young children. This is rare, but do watch your baby closely, especially if there is a family history of allergies or conditions such as eczema or asthma.

Vegetables

Your baby is now able to eat all vegetables, but if certain flavours – like that of spinach or broccoli – are too strong, try mixing them together with a cheese sauce or with root vegetables like sweet potato, carrot or potato. Combinations of vegetables and fruit are also good – try butternut squash and apple, or spinach and pear. Steamed vegetables, like carrot sticks or small florets of cauliflower, make good finger food.

Frozen vegetables reach the freezer within hours of being picked, and often retain as many nutrients as fresh ones. They are fine for making baby food and, once cooked, can be refrozen.

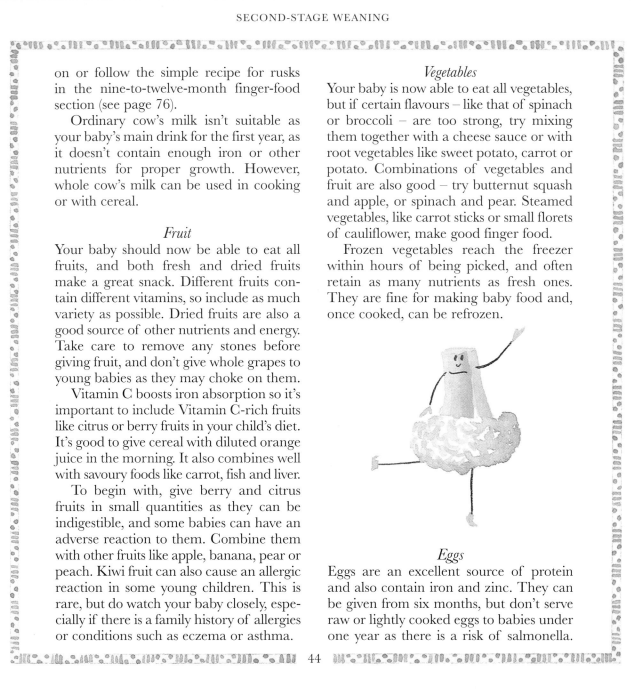

Eggs

Eggs are an excellent source of protein and also contain iron and zinc. They can be given from six months, but don't serve raw or lightly cooked eggs to babies under one year as there is a risk of salmonella.

The white and yolk should be cooked until solid. Hard-boiled eggs, omelettes and well-cooked scrambled eggs are quick to cook and nutritious.

Fish

Many children grow up disliking fish as they find it bland and boring. Counteract this by mixing it with stronger tastes like cheese or tomato. If your child gets excited at the prospect of fish for dinner, then you deserve to be a very proud parent indeed.

Oily fish like salmon, mackerel, fresh tuna and sardines are particularly important for brain and visual development. Ideally they should be included in the diet twice a week.

If fish is overcooked it becomes tough and tasteless. It is cooked when it just flakes with a fork but is still firm. Always check very carefully for bones before serving.

Meat

Chicken is an ideal first meat. It blends well with root vegetables like carrot and sweet potato, which give chicken purée a smoother texture. Chicken also works well with fruits like apple and grape. Home-made chicken stock forms the basis of many recipes so I recommend that you make large batches. It will keep in the fridge for 3–4 days.

Iron is important for brain development, and a baby requires the most iron between six months and two years. Iron deficiency anaemia is the most common nutritional problem during early childhood, the symptoms of which can be hard to detect:

your baby may just be tired and pale and more prone to infection, or his growth and development may seem to slow down. Red meat provides the best source of iron, in particular liver, which is ideal for babies as it has a soft texture and is easy to digest. Babies often reject a lot of red meats, not because of the taste but the chewy texture. It's a good idea to combine it with root vegetables or pasta, as they help to produce a texture that is much smoother and easier to swallow.

Pasta

Pasta tends to be a favourite with babies and young children. It's a good source of carbohydrate and adding tiny pasta shapes to purées when your baby is about eight months is a good way to encourage chewing. Many vegetable purées make good pasta sauces, to which you could add a little grated cheese. Either buy tiny pasta shapes or chop up spaghetti. Also try couscous, which has a soft texture perfect for babies. It is quick to cook and combines well with diced chicken or vegetables.

TEXTURES

You shouldn't give smooth purées to your baby for too long as it is important that he learns to chew. As teeth begin to emerge, give coarser purées and grated, mashed and finely chopped food. Initially, babies often refuse to eat food that has lumps in it. If this happens, try adding pasta to purées as mentioned above, or give tender steamed vegetables or fruit as finger food.

FRUIT

Going Bananas

Babies love bananas and this recipe makes them taste truly scrumptious.
Delicious with vanilla ice cream.

MAKES 1 PORTION

a knob of butter *a pinch of ground cinnamon*
1 small banana, peeled and sliced *2 tablespoons freshly squeezed orange juice*

Melt the butter in a small frying pan, stir in the sliced banana, sprinkle
with a little cinnamon and sauté for 2 minutes. Pour in the orange
juice and continue to cook for another 2 minutes. Mash with a fork.

Banana and Blueberry

Bananas combine well with lots of different fruits. Try, also, peach,
mango, dried apricot or prune. You can also mix banana and fruit combinations with some full-fat natural yoghurt. Serve straight away, before
the banana turns brown.

MAKES 1 PORTION

25 g / 1 oz blueberries *1 small ripe banana, peeled and sliced*
1 tablespoon water

Put the blueberries into a saucepan with the water and cook for about
2 minutes or until the fruit just starts to burst open. Whiz with a hand
blender, together with the sliced banana, until smooth.

Peach, Apple and Strawberry Purée

You could also make Apple, Strawberry and Blueberry Purée using 25 g/
1 oz blueberries instead of peach.

MAKES 2 PORTIONS

1 large apple, peeled, cored and chopped
1 large ripe peach, peeled, stoned and
chopped

75 g/3 oz strawberries, halved
1 tablespoon baby rice

S team the apple for about 4 minutes. Add the peach and strawberries to
the steamer and continue to cook for about 3 minutes. Blend the fruits
to a smooth purée and stir in the baby rice.

Peaches and Rice

You could also combine the cooked rice with other fruits like dried apricots (chop, and simmer with the rice), or plums cooked with a little sugar.

MAKES 2 PORTIONS

1 tablespoon flaked rice
150 ml/5 fl oz milk
1 ripe peach, stoned, skinned and chopped

P ut the rice and milk in a small
saucepan. Stir over a low heat
for about 5 minutes or until it boils
and thickens. Simmer for 5 minutes, then stir in the chopped
peach. Purée for young babies.

Apricot, Apple and Peach Purée

Dried apricots are a concentrated source of nutrients, they are rich in iron, potassium and betacarotene, and babies tend to like their sweet flavour.

MAKES 5 PORTIONS

75 g/3 oz ready-to-eat dried apricots
2 apples, peeled, cored and chopped

1 large ripe peach, skinned, stoned and chopped, or 1 ripe pear, peeled, cored and chopped

Put the apricots into a small saucepan and cover with water. Cook over a low heat for 5 minutes. Add the chopped apples and continue to cook for 5 minutes. Purée together with the peach or pear.

Yoghurt and Fruit

It's important to make sure that as well as fruit and vegetables, your baby gets enough fat in his diet. Recipes like vegetables in cheese sauce and fruit mixes with Greek yoghurt are very good for your baby.

MAKES 1 PORTION

fresh fruit, e.g. 1 ripe peach, small mango or a combination like mango and banana

2 tablespoons full-fat natural yoghurt
a little maple syrup (optional)

Peel the fruit, remove any stones, mash the flesh and mix with the yoghurt. Stir in a little maple syrup to sweeten if necessary.

Home-Made Fruit Jelly

It's easy to make jelly with delicious fruit juices and fresh fruit. Personally, I prefer to use 4 sheets of leaf gelatine rather than gelatine powder (see method below), so I would recommend you try this.

MAKES 4 PORTIONS

600 ml / 1 pint cranberry and raspberry juice   *2 tablespoons caster sugar*
1 sachet gelatine powder   *125 g / 4½ oz fresh raspberries*

Place half of the juice in a small saucepan and heat until just at boiling point. Remove from the heat and stir in the gelatine and caster sugar until dissolved. If not completely dissolved, stir over a low heat but do not boil. Pour this into the remaining cold juice and then pour into a serving dish and stir in the raspberries. Refrigerate until set.

Blood Orange Jelly

Leaf gelatine dissolves like a dream and is fantastic for making jelly.

MAKES 4 PORTIONS

4 leaves gelatine   *blood orange juice*
600 ml / 1 pint freshly squeezed   *3 tablespoons caster sugar*

Break the gelatine leaves into a roasting tin or shallow dish (use 6 leaves if using a mould). Pour over 6 tablespoons juice. Heat the rest of the juice until very hot but not boiling and stir in the sugar until dissolved. Remove from the heat. Little by little, take the softened gelatine out of the tin and stir into the hot juice. The gelatine will disappear. Stir in any juice left in the tin. Leave to cool. Pour the juice into a bowl, individual glasses or jelly mould. Chill until set.

VEGETABLES
Lovely Lentils

Lentils are a good cheap source of protein. They also provide iron, which is very important for brain development particularly between the ages of six months and two years. Lentils can be difficult for young babies to digest and should be combined with plenty of fresh vegetables as in this recipe. This tasty purée also makes a delicious soup for the family by simply adding more stock and some seasoning.

MAKES 8 PORTIONS

½ small onion, finely chopped
100 g/4 oz carrot, chopped
15 g/½ oz celery, chopped
1 tablespoon vegetable oil
50 g/2 oz split red lentils

200 g/7 oz sweet potato, peeled and chopped
400 ml/14 fl oz vegetable or chicken stock (see page 33 or 62) or water

Sauté the onion, carrot and celery in the vegetable oil for about 5 minutes or until softened. Add the lentils and sweet potato and pour over the stock or water. Bring to the boil, turn down the heat and simmer covered for 20 minutes. Purée in a blender.

Tomatoes and Carrots with Basil

If you introduce your baby to new flavours at an early age, he will tend to grow up a less fussy eater.

MAKES 4 PORTIONS

125 g/4½ oz carrots, peeled and sliced
100 g/4 oz cauliflower, cut into florets
25 g/1 oz butter

200 g/7 oz ripe tomatoes, skinned,
deseeded and roughly chopped
2–3 fresh basil leaves
50 g/2 oz Cheddar cheese, grated

Put the carrots in a small saucepan, cover with boiling water and simmer, covered, for 10 minutes. Add the cauliflower and cook, covered, for 7–8 minutes, adding extra water if necessary. Meanwhile, melt the butter, add the tomatoes and sauté until mushy. Stir in the basil and cheese until melted. Purée the carrots and cauliflower with about 3 tablespoons of the cooking liquid and the tomato sauce.

Baked Sweet Potato with Orange

Sweet potatoes are delicious baked like jacket potatoes either in the oven or microwave and then combined with fruit like apple or peach purée. They are a good source of carbohydrate, vitamins and minerals.

MAKES 8 PORTIONS

1 medium sweet potato, scrubbed
2 tablespoons freshly squeezed orange juice

2 tablespoons milk

Cook the sweet potato on a baking sheet in an oven preheated to 200°C/ 400°F/Gas 6 for about 1 hour or until tender. Cool a little, then scoop out the flesh. Purée or mash with the orange juice and milk until smooth.

Sweet Potato with Spinach and Peas

This purée makes a tasty introduction to spinach for your baby.

MAKES 5 PORTIONS

20 g/¾ oz butter
50 g/2 oz leek, finely sliced
1 sweet potato (about 375 g/13 oz),
peeled and chopped

200 ml/7 fl oz water
50 g/2 oz frozen peas
75 g/3 oz fresh baby spinach, washed
and any tough stalks removed

Melt the butter in a saucepan and sauté the leek for 2–3 minutes or until softened. Add the sweet potato. Pour over the water, bring to the boil, then cover and simmer for 7–8 minutes. Add the peas and spinach and cook for 3 minutes. Purée the vegetables in a blender to make a smooth consistency for your baby.

Sweet Vegetable Purée

Whilst vegetables like peas and sweetcorn have a sweet taste that babies like, they should be puréed in a mouli as the husks are indigestible.

MAKES 3 PORTIONS

25 g/1 oz chopped onion
75 g/3 oz carrot, peeled and chopped
1 tablespoon olive oil
150 g/5 oz potato, peeled and chopped

200 ml/7 fl oz water
2 tablespoons frozen sweetcorn
1 tablespoon frozen peas

Fry the onion and carrot gently in the oil over for 5 minutes. Stir in the potato, add the water, bring to the boil, then cover and simmer for 10 minutes. Add the sweetcorn and peas and simmer for about 5 minutes. Purée in a mouli.

Trio of Cauliflower, Red Pepper and Sweetcorn

Babies like the bright colour and natural sweetness of these vegetables. Always purée sweetcorn in a mouli for young babies, to get rid of the tough outer skin.

MAKES 4 PORTIONS

100 g / 4 oz cauliflower, broken into small florets
120 ml / 1 fl oz milk

50 g / 2 oz grated Cheddar cheese
25 g / 1 oz sweet red pepper, chopped
75 g / 3 oz frozen sweetcorn

Put the cauliflower in a small saucepan with the milk and cook over a low heat for about 8 minutes until tender. Stir in the grated cheese until melted. Meanwhile, steam the red pepper and sweetcorn or cook in some water in a small saucepan for about 6 minutes until tender. Drain the sweetcorn and pepper. Purée together with the cauliflower milk and cheese in a mouli.

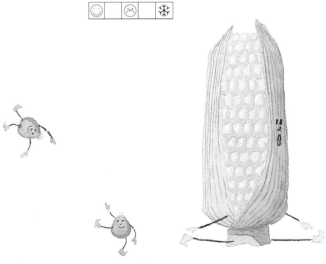

Cauliflower Cheese

This is a great favourite with babies. Try using different cheeses or combinations of cheese until you find your baby's favourite taste. The cheese sauce can be used over a mixture of vegetables as well.

MAKES 5 PORTIONS

175 g / 6 oz cauliflower

Cheese Sauce
15g / ½ oz butter
1 tablespoon plain flour
150 ml / 5 fl oz milk
50 g / 2 oz Cheddar, Edam or Gruyère cheese, grated

Wash the cauliflower carefully, divide it into small florets and steam until tender (about 10 minutes). Meanwhile, for the sauce, melt the butter over a low heat in a heavy-bottomed saucepan and stir in the flour to make a smooth paste. Whisk in the milk and stir until thickened. Take the saucepan off the heat and stir in the grated cheese. Keep stirring until all the cheese has melted and the sauce is smooth.

Add the cauliflower to the sauce and purée in a blender for younger babies. For older babies, mash with a fork or chop into little pieces.

Courgette Gratin

This creamy purée is also good using broccoli.

MAKES 6 PORTIONS

*1 medium potato (about 100 g/4 oz),
peeled and chopped
175 g/6 oz courgettes, sliced*

*a knob of butter
40 g/1½ oz Cheddar or Gruyère cheese
4 tablespoons milk*

Boil the potato until soft. Steam the courgettes for 8 minutes. Drain the potatoes, add the butter and cheese and stir until melted. Purée the potato mixture, courgettes and milk with an electric hand blender.

Leek and Potato Purée

This was Lara's favourite vegetable purée. It also makes a delicious soup for adults if you add seasoning.

MAKES 4 PORTIONS

*25 g/1 oz butter
125 g/4½ oz leeks, finely sliced
250 g/9 oz potatoes, peeled and chopped*

*300 ml/10 fl oz chicken or vegetable
stock (see page 62 or 33)
2 tablespoons Greek yoghurt*

Heat the butter in a saucepan. Add the leeks and cook over a low heat for 5 minutes. Add the potatoes and pour over the stock. Cover and cook for about 12 minutes or until tender. Strain the vegetables and purée in a mouli adding as much of the cooking liquid as necessary to make a smooth consistency. Stir in the yoghurt.

Courgette and Pea Souper

When I experimented with this combination, the baby purée turned out to be so good that I also made a delicious soup for the rest of the family. Simply increase the quantities and add extra stock and seasoning.

MAKES 4 PORTIONS

½ small onion, peeled and finely chopped
15 g/½ oz butter or margarine
50 g/2 oz courgette, trimmed and thinly sliced

1 medium potato (about 150 g/5 oz), peeled and chopped
120 ml/4 fl oz chicken or vegetable stock (see page 62 or 33)
25 g/1 oz frozen peas

Sauté the onion in the butter or margarine until softened. Add the courgette, potato and stock. Bring to the boil, then cover and simmer for 12 minutes. Add the frozen peas, bring to the boil, then reduce the heat and continue to cook for 5 minutes. Purée in a blender.

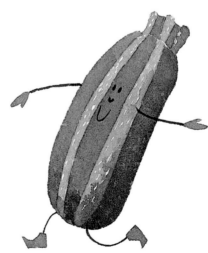

Minestrone

The vegetables in minestrone soup add texture but are nice and soft for your baby to chew. However, for younger babies you could blend this soup to the desired texture. Add a little seasoning and some extra stock to make this into a delicious soup for the rest of the family.

MAKES 4 ADULT PORTIONS OR 12 BABY PORTIONS

1 tablespoon vegetable oil
½ small onion, finely chopped
½ leek, white part only, washed and finely chopped
1 medium carrot, peeled and diced
½ celery stalk, diced
100 g / 4 oz French beans, cut into 1 cm / ½ inch lengths

1 potato, peeled and diced
1 tablespoon fresh parsley, finely chopped
2 teaspoons tomato purée
1.2 litres / 2 pints chicken or vegetable stock (see pages 62 and 33)
3 tablespoons frozen peas
50 g / 2 oz very small pasta shapes

Heat the oil in a saucepan and fry the onion and leek for 2 minutes, then add the carrot, celery, French beans, potato and parsley and sauté for 4 minutes. Stir in the tomato purée and cook for 1 minute. Pour over the chicken or vegetable stock and simmer, covered, for 20 minutes. Add the frozen peas and pasta and cook for 5 minutes (check the packet instructions for the cooking time of pasta).

FISH

Plaice with Tomatoes and Potato

This makes a good, creamy-textured fish purée.

MAKES 4 PORTIONS

1 fillet of plaice, skinned
2 medium tomatoes, skinned, deseeded
and chopped
a little margarine or butter

1 bay leaf
150 ml/5 fl oz milk
1 small potato, peeled

Put the plaice into a dish, cover with the chopped tomato, dot with a little margarine or butter and add the bay leaf. Pour over most of the milk. Cover with foil and cook in an oven preheated to 180°C/350°F/ Gas 4, for 20 minutes. (Alternatively, cover with a lid and cook in the microwave on High for about 3 minutes.)

Whilst the fish is cooking, boil the potato. When soft, mash it with the remaining milk and margarine or butter. Flake the fish when it is cooked, remove the bay leaf and mash or purée the fish together with the liquid in which it was cooked. You can either mix in the mashed potato or serve it as an accompaniment to the fish.

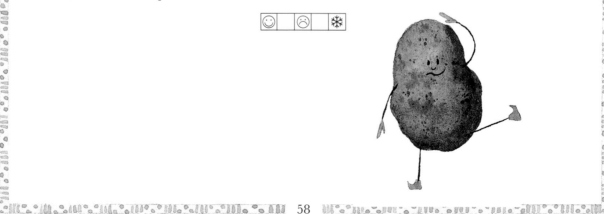

Fillets of Fish in Cheese Sauce

Fish and cheese sauce go really well together and the combination is always popular. Add some chives and you give an old recipe a new taste.

MAKES 6 PORTIONS

175 g / 6 oz cod, plaice or hake, filleted
and skinned
3 tablespoons milk
1 bay leaf
a knob of butter

Cheese Sauce
20 g / ¾ oz butter
2 tablespoons plain flour
175 ml / 6 fl oz milk
65 g / 2½ oz Cheddar cheese, grated
1 teaspoon fresh parsley or chives,
chopped

Put the fish in a suitable dish together with the milk and bay leaf and dot with butter. Cover and microwave on High for about 4 minutes. Alternatively, poach the fish in milk in a saucepan until cooked.

To prepare the sauce, melt the butter and stir in the flour to make a roux. Gradually whisk in the milk, cooking over a low heat until you have a smooth white sauce. Allow the sauce to come to the boil and simmer for 1 minute, stirring constantly. Take the saucepan off the heat and whisk in the cheese until melted. Add the parsley or chives.

Flake the fish with a fork, checking to make sure there are no stray bones. Mix together the flaked fish and cheese sauce and mash or purée in a blender.

Plaice with Spinach and Cheese

Frozen vegetables are a good alternative to fresh, and can often be more nutritious than vegetables that have been in the kitchen for several days. It also means you can make this when fresh spinach is not available.

MAKES 8 PORTIONS

225 g/8 oz plaice fillets, skinned
1 tablespoon milk
1 bay leaf
a few peppercorns
a knob of butter
175 g/6 oz fresh or 75 g/3 oz frozen spinach

Cheese Sauce
25 g/1 oz butter
2 tablespoons plain flour
175 ml/6 fl oz milk
50 g/2 oz Gruyère cheese

Put the plaice in a suitable dish with the milk, bay leaf, peppercorns and butter. Microwave for about 3 minutes on High or poach in a saucepan for 5 minutes. Meanwhile, cook the spinach in a saucepan with just a little water clinging to the leaves for about 3 minutes or cook frozen spinach following the packet instructions. Squeeze out the excess water. Make the cheese sauce (see page 59). Discard the bay leaf and peppercorns, flake the fish carefully and purée with the spinach and cheese sauce to the desired consistency.

Fillet of Cod with Sweet Potato

The orange-fleshed sweet potato is an excellent source of betacarotene, which may help to prevent certain types of cancer. Babies tend to love the taste of sweet potato, so this recipe makes a good introduction to fish.

MAKES 8 PORTIONS

225 g/8 oz sweet potato, peeled
75 g/3 oz cod, skinned and filleted
2 tablespoons milk

a knob of butter
juice of 1 orange (about 120 ml/4 fl oz)

Put the sweet potato into a saucepan, just cover with water, bring to the boil, then cover and simmer for 20 minutes or until soft. Put the fish in a suitable dish, add the milk, dot with butter, cover and microwave on High for 2 minutes or until the fish is cooked. Alternatively, poach the fish in a saucepan with the milk and butter for 6–7 minutes or until just cooked through. Put the cooked sweet potato, drained fish and orange juice into a blender and purée until smooth.

Fillet of Fish in an Orange Sauce

This is one of my family's favourite fish recipes. Do not be put off by the odd combination, as it gives a marvellous rich taste.

MAKES 5 PORTIONS

225 g / 8 oz fillet of fish, skinned, e.g. cod, haddock or hake
juice of 1 orange (about 120 ml / 4 fl oz)
40 g / 1½ oz Cheddar cheese, grated

1 dessertspoon fresh parsley, finely chopped
25 g / 1 oz crushed cornflakes
7 g / ¼ oz margarine

Put the haddock in a greased dish, cover with the orange juice, cheese, parsley and cornflakes and dot with the margarine. Cover with foil and bake in an oven pre-heated to 180°C/350°F/Gas 4 for about 20 minutes. Alternatively, cover with a lid and cook in a microwave on High for 4 minutes.

Flake the fish carefully, removing any bones, and mash everything together with the liquid in which the fish was cooked.

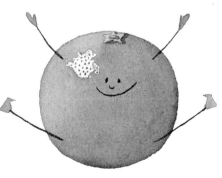

CHICKEN

Chicken Stock and My First Chicken Purée

Stock cubes are unsuitable for babies under a year as they are high in salt, so I make my own chicken stock and use it as a base for chicken and vegetable purées. It keeps in the fridge for 3 days. For babies over one year you can add 3 chicken stock cubes for a stronger flavour. Instead of a boiler chicken, you could use the carcass from a roast chicken.

MAKES APPROXIMATELY 2¼ LITRES/4 PINTS

1 large boiler chicken, plus giblets
2¼ litres/4 pints water
2 parsnips
3 large carrots
2 leeks

2 large onions
1 celery stalk
2 sprigs of fresh parsley
1 sachet bouquet garni

Cut the chicken into eight pieces, trimming excess fat. Trim, peel, wash and chop the vegetables as necessary. Put the chicken pieces into a large saucepan together with the giblets. Cover with the water, bring to the boil and skim the froth from the top. Add the remaining ingredients and simmer for about 3 hours. It is best to remove the chicken breasts after about 1½ hours if you are going to eat them; otherwise they will become too dry.

Leave the soup in the fridge overnight and remove any congealed fat from the top in the morning. Strain out all the chicken and vegetables to make the chicken stock.

You can purée some of the chicken breast in a mouli, together with a selection of the vegetables and some stock to make a chicken and vegetable purée. This also makes a wonderful clear chicken soup (with added stock cubes and seasoning) for older babies and you can add some thin noodles.

Chicken with Cottage Cheese

Babies of this age are a little too young to eat pieces of chicken as finger
food. This and the following three recipes show you simple ways of
transforming cold chicken into tasty food for your baby.

MAKES 2 PORTIONS

50 g / 2 oz cooked boneless chicken,
chopped
1 tablespoon natural yoghurt

1½ tablespoons cottage cheese with
pineapple

Mix together the chicken, yoghurt and cottage cheese. Blend to the
desired consistency.

Chicken with Parsnip and Beans

If freezing this recipe, do not purée the chicken with the vegetables until
they are cold. It is important to avoid warming the chicken.

MAKES 5 PORTIONS

50 g / 2 oz parsnip, peeled and sliced
100 g / 4 oz sweet potato, peeled and
chopped
25 g / 1 oz green beans, topped and tailed

40 g / 1½ oz cooked boneless chicken
1 tablespoons chicken stock
(see page 62) or milk

Put the vegetables into a saucepan, cover with water, bring to the boil,
then cover and simmer until tender. Drain,
then purée with the chicken and the stock or milk.

Chicken with Sweet Potato and Apple

This combination gives a smooth texture and sweet taste that babies like.

MAKES 4 PORTIONS

15 g/½ oz butter
40 g/1½ oz onion, chopped
100 g/4 oz chicken breast, chopped
½ dessert apple, peeled and chopped

1 sweet potato (about 300 g/11 oz),
peeled and chopped
200 ml/7 fl oz chicken stock (see
page 62)

Melt the butter in a saucepan, add the onion and sauté for 2–3 minutes. Add the chicken and sauté until it turns opaque. Add the apple, sweet potato and stock. Bring to the boil, cover and simmer for 15 minutes. Purée to the desired consistency.

Chicken Salad Purée

What could be simpler? For toddlers, simply chop the ingredients, leave out the yoghurt and mix with mayonnaise or salad cream.

MAKES 1 PORTION

25 g/1 oz cooked boneless chicken
1 slice cucumber, peeled and chopped
1 small tomato, skinned, deseeded and
chopped
50 g/2 oz avocado, peeled and chopped
1 tablespoon mild natural yoghurt

Put all the ingredients into a blender and purée until the desired consistency. Serve immediately.

Chicken in Tomato Sauce

MAKES 12 PORTIONS

25 g/1 oz chopped onion
100 g/4 oz carrot, thinly sliced
1½ tablespoons vegetable oil
1 small chicken breast, cut into chunks

100 g/4 oz potato, peeled and chopped
200 g/7 oz canned chopped tomatoes
150 ml/5 fl oz chicken stock (see page 62)

Sauté the onion and carrot in the vegetable oil until softened, then add the chicken and potato and continue to cook for 3 minutes. Pour over the chopped tomatoes together with the chicken stock. Bring to the boil and cook over a low heat for about 30 minutes or until the potato is quite soft. Put the mixture through a mouli or, for babies of nine months and older, chop in a blender. You could also add a little milk to make a smoother texture if you wish.

Easy One-Pot Chicken

This is an ideal purée for introducing young babies to chicken.

MAKES 12 PORTIONS

½ small onion, peeled and chopped
15 g/½ oz butter
100 g/4 oz chicken breast, cut into chunks
1 medium carrot, peeled and sliced

275 g/10 oz sweet potato, peeled and chopped
300 ml/10 fl oz chicken stock (see page 62)

Sauté the onion in the butter until softened. Add the chicken breast and sauté for 3–4 minutes. Add the vegetables, pour over the stock, bring to the boil and simmer, covered, for about 30 minutes or until the chicken is cooked through and the vegetables are tender. Purée in a blender to the desired consistency.

Chicken with Grapes and Courgette

The addition of grapes to this recipe gives the chicken a little sweetness, which babies love. It is very simple to make and is usually gobbled up pretty quickly.

MAKES 4 PORTIONS

1 chicken breast or 2 chicken thighs, skinned and off the bone
150 ml / 5 fl oz chicken stock (see page 62)

8 white grapes, peeled and deseeded
1 courgette, trimmed and sliced
1 tablespoon baby rice

Cut the chicken into small pieces. Put all the ingredients except the baby rice into a small saucepan, bring to the boil and simmer for 10 minutes. Purée to the desired consistency and thicken by stirring in the baby rice.

RED MEATS

Braised Beef with Sweet Potato

Both this and the recipe below make good introductions to red meat.

MAKES 6 PORTIONS

1 leek, washed and sliced
20 g/¾ oz butter
100 g/4 oz braising steak or lamb, cut into cubes
2 tablespoons flour

275 g/10 oz sweet potato, peeled and chopped
300 ml/10 fl oz chicken stock (see page 62)
juice of 1 orange (about 120 ml/4 fl oz)

In a flameproof casserole, soften the leek in the butter. Roll the meat in the flour and add to the leek to brown. Add the sweet potato, stock and orange juice. Bring to the boil, cover and transfer to an oven preheated to 180°C/350°F/Gas 4 for 1¼ hours or until the meat is tender. Blend to the desired consistency.

Liver Special

MAKES 6 PORTIONS

75 g/3 oz calf's liver, or 2 chicken livers
120 ml/4 fl oz chicken stock (see page 62)
25 g/1 oz leek, white part only, chopped
25 g/1 oz mushrooms, chopped

50 g/2 oz carrot, chopped
1 potato, peeled and chopped
a knob of butter
½ tablespoon milk

Trim and chop the liver and cook in the stock with the leek, mushrooms and carrot for about 8 minutes over a low heat. Boil the potato until tender and mash with the butter and milk. Purée the liver and vegetables and mix with the potato.

PASTA

Tomato and Courgette Pasta Stars

This tasty pasta sauce takes only about 10 minutes to prepare.

MAKES 3 PORTIONS

25 g/1 oz pasta stars, uncooked
75 g/3 oz courgette, trimmed and diced
25 g/1 oz butter

3 medium tomatoes (about 200 g/
7 oz), skinned, deseeded and chopped
25 g/1 oz Cheddar cheese, grated

Cook the pasta according to the packet instructions, or longer for young babies. Sauté the courgette in the butter for about 5 minutes. Add the tomatoes and cook over a low heat for 5 minutes. Remove from the heat and stir in the cheese until melted. Purée in a blender and stir in the pasta.

Vegetable and Cheese Pasta Sauce

MAKES 3 PORTIONS OF SAUCE

65 g/2½ oz carrot, peeled and sliced
40 g/1½ oz broccoli florets
25 g/1 oz butter

2 tablespoons plain flour
175 ml/6 fl oz milk
40 g/1½ oz grated Cheddar cheese

Steam the carrot for 10 minutes, then add the broccoli florets and cook for 7 minutes more. Meanwhile, melt the butter in a small saucepan and stir in the flour to make a thick paste. Gradually add the milk, bring to the boil and stir continuously until the sauce thickens. Simmer for 1 minute. Remove from the heat and stir in the grated cheese. Add the cooked vegetables to the cheese sauce and blend to a purée. Serve with tiny cooked pasta shapes.

My First Bolognese Sauce

A tasty recipe to encourage your baby to enjoy eating red meat.

MAKES 3 PORTIONS

1 tablespoon olive oil
1 small onion, peeled and chopped
1 garlic clove, crushed
1 medium carrot, peeled and grated
½ celery stalk, finely chopped

100 g / 4 oz lean minced beef
3 medium tomatoes, skinned and chopped
½ teaspoon tomato purée
150 ml / 5 fl oz unsalted chicken stock
3 tablespoons tiny pasta shapes

Heat the oil and sauté the onion, garlic, carrot and celery for 5 minutes. Add the minced beef and sauté until browned, stirring occasionally. Stir in the tomatoes, tomato purée and chicken stock. Bring to the boil, then simmer for 15 minutes. Meanwhile, cook the pasta shapes according to the packet directions. Transfer the sauce to a blender and purée to a fairly smooth consistency. Drain the pasta and mix with the sauce.

Tomato and Basil Pasta Sauce

Butterfly-shaped pasta is fun for babies to grasp in their hands.

MAKES 2 PORTIONS OF SAUCE

15 g / ½ oz butter
2 tablespoons chopped onion
150 g / 5 oz ripe tomatoes, skinned,

deseeded and chopped
2 fresh basil leaves, torn
2 teaspoons cream cheese

Melt the butter in a saucepan and sauté the onion until softened. Add the tomatoes and sauté for 3 minutes or until mushy. Stir in the basil and cream cheese and heat through. Purée in a blender.

Napolitana Pasta Sauce

A tasty tomato sauce which goes well with all types of pasta – my children love this with ravioli stuffed with ricotta and spinach.

MAKES 4 PORTIONS OF SAUCE

1 tablespoon olive oil
½ small onion, peeled and chopped
½ garlic clove, peeled and crushed
50 g / 2 oz carrot, peeled and chopped
200 ml / 7 fl oz passata

3 tablespoons water
2 fresh basil leaves, roughly torn
1 teaspoon grated Parmesan cheese
1 teaspoon cream cheese

Heat the olive oil and sauté the onion, garlic and carrot for 6 minutes. Add the passata, water, basil and Parmesan. Cover and simmer for 15 minutes. Purée the sauce and stir in the cream cheese. Mix with pasta and serve.

Popeye Pasta

MAKES 4 PORTIONS

100 g / 4 oz frozen or 225 g / 8 oz fresh spinach, washed
50 g / 2 oz tiny pasta shapes (like soup pasta), uncooked

15 g / ½ oz butter
2 tablespoons milk
2 tablespoons cream cheese
40 g / 1½ oz Gruyère cheese, grated

Cook the spinach according to the packet instructions or, if fresh, with just the water clinging to its leaves in a microwave or in a saucepan over a low heat until tender. Press out the excess water. Cook the pasta according to the packet instructions. Meanwhile, melt the butter in a small frying pan and sauté the cooked spinach. Combine the spinach with the milk and cheeses, and chop finely in a food processor. Mix with the cooked pasta.

SECOND-STAGE WEANING MEAL PLANNER

	Breakfast	Mid-morning	Lunch	Mid-afternoon	Tea	Bedtime
Day 1	Weetabix with milk Mashed banana	Milk	**My First Chicken Purée** Grated apple Juice	Milk	**Leek and Potato Purée** Pear purée Water or juice	Milk
Day 2	Ready Brek or porridge with milk Fruit purée Milk	Milk	**Plaice with Tomatoes and Potato** Mashed banana Juice	Milk	**Courgette and Pea Souper** Yoghurt Water or juice	Milk
Day 3	Apple purée and baby cereal Toast Milk	Milk	**Cauliflower Cheese** Grated pear Juice	Milk	**Braised Beef with Sweet Potato** Rusk Water or juice	Milk
Day 4	Baby cereal with milk Dried apricot purée Fromage frais	Milk	**Lovely Lentils** **Peaches and Rice** Juice	Milk	**Minestrone** Toast Water or juice	Milk
Day 5	Weetabix with milk **Peach, Apple and Strawberry Purée**	Milk	Pasta with **Vegetable and Cheese Pasta Sauce** **Going Bananas** Juice	Milk	**My First Bolognese Sauce** Pear purée Water or juice	Milk
Day 6	Baby cereal with milk **Peach, Apple and Strawberry Purée**	Milk	**Tomatoes and Carrots with Basil** **Home-Made Fruit Jelly** Juice	Milk	**Fillet of Fish in an Orange Sauce** Apple Water	Milk
Day 7	Ready Brek with milk **Yoghurt and Fruit**	Milk	**Sweet Potato with Spinach and Peas** **Apricot, Apple and Peach Purée** Juice	Milk	**Easy One-Pot Chicken** Papaya purée Water or juice	Milk

CHAPTER FOUR

NINE TO TWELVE MONTHS

Towards the end of the first year, a baby's weight gain usually slows down quite dramatically. Often babies who have been good eaters in the past become much more difficult to feed. Many refuse to be spoon-fed and want to assert their new-found independence, using their hands to feed themselves. My older daughter at the age of ten months went through a phase of refusing to eat anything offered to her on a spoon. I was determined that she should eat the home-made purées I had prepared, so I gave her various finger foods like steamed carrots or strips of toast, which I dipped into the purées. That way I succeeded in getting her to eat and enjoy them, and everyone was happy.

MEALTIME PATIENCE

Let your baby experiment by allowing her to use a spoon. Most of the food will probably end up on you or on the floor, but the more you allow your baby to experiment, the quicker she will master the art of feeding herself. Put a plastic splash mat under the high chair to catch the food that falls on the floor so that you can recycle it. It is probably best to have two bowls of food and two spoons; one which you use to spoon-feed your baby, the other (preferably a bowl which sticks to the table by suction) for your baby to play with. You will need lots of patience at mealtimes, as many babies are very easily distracted at this stage and prefer to play with their food rather than eat it. If all else fails, I find that if you can attract their attention by giving them a small toy to hold, you can sometimes slip food into their mouths on a spoon and they will eat without really noticing what they are doing and forget to put up any resistance!

Continue giving breast or formula milk as your baby's main drink. Cow's milk is not suitable as a main drink because it is low in essential vitamins and minerals like iron. However, as solid-food intake increases, milk need no longer form such a staple part of your child's diet, although they should still be drinking about 500 ml/18 fl oz of milk a day (or the equivalent as dairy products or in cooking). It is an important source of protein and calcium. Many mothers assume that when their baby cries it is because she wants more milk, but often babies of this age are given *too much* milk and not enough solid food. If you fill your baby's stomach with milk when she really wants some solid food, you will not get a very satisfied baby.

If you have a juice extractor, you can make all sorts of wonderful fruit and vegetable drinks for your baby – try combinations like apple, strawberry and banana. Your baby should now be drinking happily from a cup, the bottle kept for her bedtime drink of warm milk.

Your baby will be teething at this age and very often sore gums can put her off eating for a while. Don't worry, as she will make up for this later that day or the next day. (Rubbing a teething gel on your baby's gums, or giving her something very cold to chew, can help relieve soreness and restore appetite.)

It is a good idea to eat something with your baby at mealtimes. There are some mothers who sit opposite their babies and try to spoon food into their mouths whilst eating nothing themselves. Babies are great mimics and will be much more likely to enjoy eating if they see you tucking in as well.

THE FOODS TO CHOOSE

Now you can be a little more adventurous with the food that you make for your baby. It is a good idea to develop her tastes for garlic and herbs, both of which are very healthy. Children tend to be less fussy eaters if they are introduced to a wide range of foods early. Again, if your baby dislikes certain foods, never force her to eat them; just leave out those foods and perhaps reintroduce them in a couple of days' time. Try also to vary the foods as much as possible, as this will lead to a more balanced diet. If you give your child a favourite food too often, it is possible she will go off it altogether.

Your baby can now eat berry fruits (but these should still be put through a mouli in the earlier stages to get rid of the indigestible seeds). Fruit jellies will be interesting for your baby to look at, feel and eat. Your baby should also like fruit and vegetables that have been grated. Oily fish like salmon, sardines and fresh tuna contains essential fatty acids and iron so it is particularly good for your child. All fish must obviously be very fresh. Chicken dishes can become more interesting in both texture and tastes and the types of pasta cooked can be large enough for the independent baby to pick up (butterflies, spirals, shells and animal shapes are good). Increase the quantity per serving of pasta to about 40 g/1½ oz cooked (15–20 g/ ½–¾ oz dry).

When possible, try to make your baby's food look attractive on the plate. Choose contrasting colours and arrange the food in pretty shapes. You can use your imagination to make little faces or animals. Never pile too much food onto the plate, but make enough to give a second helping – your baby will let you know in no uncertain terms if she wants more.

Meat

Red meat is good for young children as it provides the best source of iron. If using fresh mince choose good-quality meat and ask your butcher to mince it for you rather than buying it ready prepared. After cooking mince for young babies, I find that if I chop it in a food processor for 30 seconds, it becomes softer and easier to chew. It's best not to give sausages or other processed meats to children, like pâté or meat pies.

TEXTURES AND QUANTITIES

It is easy to get into the habit of only giving your baby soft foods, but you should try to vary the consistency of the food you give to your baby. There is no need to purée all foods. Babies do not need teeth to be able to chew; gums do a great job on foods that are not too hard. Give some food mashed (fish), some grated (cheese), some diced (carrots) and some whole (pieces of chicken, slices of toast and pieces of raw fruit).

As far as quantities are concerned, you must let your baby's appetite be your guide. You can start to freeze food in larger plastic containers and freeze individual portions like mini shepherd's pies in small ramekin dishes. Many meals in this chapter can be enjoyed by the whole family, in which case adult-sized portions are given.

FINGER FOODS

By the age of nine months, your baby will probably want to start feeding herself. It is a good idea, therefore, to start giving her some foods that are easy to eat with her fingers. Finger foods are great for occupying your child while you prepare her meal – or you could make a whole meal of finger foods.

Never leave your child unattended whilst eating. It is very easy for a baby to choke on even very small pieces of food. Avoid giving your baby whole nuts, fruits that contain stones, whole grapes, ice cubes, olives or any other foods that might get stuck in her throat.

What To Do If Your Baby Chokes

If your baby chokes, lay her face down on your forearm or lap with her head lower than her chest. Support her head and give her five light slaps between her shoulders with your free hand.

Raw Fruit

When giving your baby fruit, make sure any pips or stones have been removed. If she finds it difficult to chew, give soft fruits that melt in the mouth such as bananas, peaches or grated fruits. Berry and citrus fruits should only be given in small quantities to start with. Remove as much pith as possible.

Many babies who are teething really enjoy biting into fruit. A banana put into the freezer for a few hours makes an excellent teething aid for young babies. Once your baby is able to hold food successfully, give her larger pieces of fruit and encourage her to bite little bits off. (But don't let her *store* these in her mouth; on occasion I had to resort to opening my son's mouth and removing food he refused to swallow!) If your baby has only a few teeth, then it is a good idea to give her grated fruit to chew.

FRUITY IDEAS

apple, apricots, avocado, banana, blueberries, cherries, clementine, grapes, kiwi fruit, mango, melon, nectarine, orange, papaya, peach, pear, plum, raspberries, strawberries, tomato

---

Dried Fruits

These are a good source of fibre, iron and energy. Choose ready-to-eat fruits that are soft. Some dried apricots are treated with sulphur dioxide to preserve their bright orange colour; these should be avoided as they can trigger an asthma attack in susceptible babies. Don't give your baby lots of dried fruit as it can be difficult to digest – and laxative.

MORE FRUITY IDEAS

apple rings, apricots, banana chips, dates, peaches, pears, prunes, raisins, sultanas

---

Vegetables

To begin with, give your baby soft cooked vegetables cut into pieces that are easy for her to hold, and encourage her to bite off little pieces. (It is best to steam vegetables as this will help to preserve Vitamin C.) Gradually cook the vegetables for less time so that your baby gets used to having to chew harder. Once your baby has good coordination, she will enjoy picking up little vegetables like peas and sweetcorn.

Once your baby has mastered the art of feeding herself cooked vegetables, you can introduce carefully washed grated raw vegetables and sticks of raw vegetables. Even if your baby is unable to bite into these sticks, she will enjoy chewing on them as an aid to teething. In fact, sticks of raw vegetables such as carrots and cucumber are very soothing for sore gums if they are chilled in the freezer or in iced water for a few minutes. Large pieces of raw vegetables are safer than small pieces as a baby will nibble off what she can manage, whereas a small piece put into her mouth whole could cause her to choke if she tried to swallow it.

Once your baby can chew well, try giving her corn on the cob. Cut the corn in half or into three pieces or look out for little mini-sized corn cobs in some supermarkets – just right for babies. Corn is fun to eat and babies love to hold and chew it.

Vegetables are also very good when dipped into sauces and purées. Try using some of the recipes for vegetable purées as dipping sauces.

VEGETABLE VARIETY

aubergine, beans (green), broccoli, butternut squash, carrots, cauliflower, celery, courgettes, mangetout, mushrooms, peas, potato, swede, sweetcorn (including corn on the cob and baby corn), sweet pepper, sweet potato

---

Breads and Rusks

Pieces of toast, rusks and firm bread, like pitta bread, can be dipped into purées and sauces. Often a baby who refuses to be spoon-fed will eat her meal by sucking it off a rusk or a piece of toast.

Many baby rusks on the market contain as much sugar as a sweet biscuit and even so-called low-sugar rusks can contain more than 15 per cent sugar. It is very easy to make your own sugar-free alternative from wholemeal bread.

HOME-MADE RUSKS

For home-made savoury rusks, simply cut a thick (1 cm/½ inch) slice of wholemeal (Granary or rye) bread into three strips. Melt ⅛ teaspoon Marmite in 1 teaspoon boiling water, and brush this evenly over the bread strips. Bake in an oven preheated to 180°C/350°F/Gas 4 for 15 minutes. Leave out the Marmite if your baby prefers and add a little grated cheese. You can prepare a store of rusks in advance and keep them in an airtight container for 3–4 days.

Rice cakes come in all different flavours and are excellent for teething, as they seem to hold together well.

Miniature Sandwiches

Little sandwiches cut into fingers, squares, small triangles or even animal shapes using a biscuit cutter are very popular with babies. Some suggestions for sandwich fillings are given below; see also the toddler section for a more exhaustive list (pages 186–87).

FILLING SUGGESTIONS

mashed banana, avocado and chopped tomato, tuna with sweetcorn and mayonnaise, cottage cheese and pineapple, cream cheese and strawberry jam, Marmite, cheese, grated cheese and tomato, mashed sardines with tomato ketchup, egg mayonnaise and salad cress

---

Breakfast Cereals

Babies love to pick up and eat little pieces of breakfast cereal. Try to choose cereals that are fortified with iron and vitamins and which do not have added sugar. Again, some suggestions are given below.

GOOD MORNING MUNCHIES

Cheerios, cornflakes, Granola, Shreddies

Cheese

Start by giving your baby grated cheese or cut wafer-thin slices. Once she has mastered chewing, you can move on to chunks and strips of cheese. I have found that the following cheeses are especially popular: Cheddar, mozzarella, Edam, Gouda, Emmenthal and Gruyère. Cream cheese and cottage cheeses are also favourites. Keep away from strong cheeses like blue cheese, Brie and Camembert. Always make sure that the cheese you give your baby is pasteurised.

Pasta

Pasta comes in all shapes and sizes, it is soft to chew and is very appealing to babies. I have given some recipes for pasta sauces but most of the vegetable purées can also be served with pasta. You can try tossing pasta in melted butter and sprinkling with grated cheese. This is usually a great favourite, even with the fussy eaters.

Meat

Slices or chunks of cooked chicken (or turkey) make great finger food. As well as plain pieces of chicken, try giving your baby chicken cooked in a sauce. Very often the sauce makes the chicken more tender and so it is easier for your baby to chew.

Miniature chicken balls are another favourite (try my recipe for Chicken and Apple Balls, page 98). Your baby may also enjoy chewing on miniature drumsticks. Remove the skin and make sure that your baby avoids eating any pieces of bone. There is a fine needle-like bone in all drumsticks that is potentially very dangerous – extra care needs to be taken.

Strips of sautéed liver make good finger food as they are easy to hold and soft to eat. Try, too, some miniature meatballs (see page 154). Pieces of steak and chunks of meat are generally too tough for young babies to chew.

Fish

Pieces of flaked white fish are good as they are low in fat, high in protein and easy for your child to chew. You can give them to your baby either plain or mixed with a sauce. Do take extra care when serving fish to your baby in any recipe to check the fish thoroughly for bones before you cook it and when flaking it.

Make your own fish fingers, fish balls and fish cakes (see pages 94, 133–34).

BREAKFAST

The first meal of the day is important for all of us after a night's fasting, particularly so for energetic babies and toddlers!

Recipes can now contain more interesting and more nutritious grains. Wheatgerm is particularly good and can be sprinkled onto cereals or yoghurt. Mixing cereals and fruit makes a delicious and nutritious start to the day. Many of the home-made cereals can be mixed with apple juice instead of milk.

Cheese is important for strong bones and teeth. You can offer cheese on toast or little strips for your baby to hold. Eggs are an excellent source of protein, vitamins and iron. Give your baby scrambled eggs or an omelette but make sure that the white and yolk are cooked until solid. Fresh fruit provides vitamins, minerals and substances called phytochemicals which help prevent cancer. Give fruit as finger foods, make fruit salads or offer stewed fruit, such as apple or rhubarb.

Highly refined, sugar-coated cereals should be avoided. Do not be fooled by the list of added vitamins on the side of the packet – unprocessed cereals are much healthier for your child.

There are also some recipes in the toddler baking and fruit dessert sections that make excellent breakfast food: Pineapple and Raisin Muffins (see page 175), Funny Shape Biscuits (see page 172) or Snow-Covered Fruit Salad (see page 165).

BREAKFAST
Fruity Swiss Muesli

This tasty and nutritious breakfast will make a good start to the day for the whole family. You can vary the fruit in the muesli, adding, for example, peaches, strawberries, bananas or ready-to-eat apricots.

MAKES 4 CHILD OR 2 ADULT PORTIONS

65 g/2½ oz rolled oats
15 g/½ oz wheat germ
175 ml/6 fl oz apple juice
1 teaspoon lemon juice

1 apple, peeled and grated
1 pear, peeled, cored and chopped
1 tablespoon maple syrup
120–150 ml/4–5 fl oz natural yoghurt

Combine the rolled oats, wheat germ and apple juice. Set aside for a couple of hours or refrigerate overnight. Next morning, mix the lemon juice with the grated apple and stir this into the oat mixture together with the chopped pear, maple syrup and yoghurt.

Fruity Yoghurt

Many commercial fruit yoghurts have a lot of added sugar. It is easy to make your own, adding a combination of your baby's favourite foods.

MAKES 2 PORTIONS

½ ripe peach stoned, skinned and chopped
½ small banana, peeled and chopped

150 ml / 5 fl oz natural yoghurt
2 teaspoons maple syrup

Simply mix all the ingredients together and serve. Mash the fruit for younger babies.

My Favourite Pancakes

Pancakes for breakfast are a treat, and this simple recipe is foolproof. Pancakes can be made in advance, refrigerated and reheated. To freeze, interleave with non-stick baking paper. Serve with maple syrup and fresh fruit.

MAKES 12 PANCAKES

100 g / 4 oz plain flour
generous pinch of salt
2 eggs

300 ml / 10 fl oz milk
50 g / 2 oz melted butter

Sift the flour and salt into a mixing bowl, make a well in the centre and add the eggs. Use a balloon whisk to incorporate the eggs into the flour and gradually whisk in the milk until just smooth.

Brush a heavy-based 15–18 cm/6–7 inch frying pan with the melted butter and when hot, pour in about 2 tablespoons of the batter. Quickly tilt the pan from side to side to form a thin layer of batter and cook for 1 minute. Flip the pancake over with a spatula and cook until the underside is slightly golden. Continue with the rest of the batter, brushing the pan with melted butter when necessary.

Apricot, Apple and Pear Custard

Dried apricots are one of nature's great health foods. They are a good concentrated source of betacarotene, potassium and iron. This tasty fruit purée works well for breakfast or dessert.

MAKES 3 PORTIONS

75 g/3 oz ready-to-eat dried apricots
1 large eating apple, peeled, cored and chopped

1 tablespoon custard powder
150 ml/5 fl oz milk
1 ripe pear, peeled, cored and chopped

Gently heat the apricots and apple in a small saucepan with 4 table spoons water for 8–10 minutes or until soft. In a saucepan, blend the custard powder with a little of the milk to make a smooth paste. Then add the remaining milk and slowly bring to the boil, stirring until thickened and smooth. Blend the cooked fruit and pear to the desired consistency and stir in the custard.

A Grown-Up Breakfast

Unfortunately many of the breakfast cereals designed specifically for children are laden with sugar. I prefer to give my children some of the more old-fashioned cereals like Weetabix, Ready Brek, Porridge or muesli and sweeten these with fresh fruit.

MAKES 1 PORTION

½ Weetabix
1 small banana

3 tablespoons mild natural yoghurt or milk

Finely crumble the Weetabix and mash the banana. Combine all the ingredients together and serve.

Summer Fruit Muesli

Simply soak the oats overnight and stir in extra fresh fruits like peaches or strawberries the next day for a tasty nutritious muesli. If your baby is too young for lumpy food, this can be blended to a fine purée.

MAKES 4 ADULT PORTIONS

100 g / 4 oz porridge oats
2 tablespoons sultanas or raisins
300 ml / 10 fl oz apple and mango juice
2 eating apples, peeled, cored and grated

4–6 tablespoons milk
a little maple syrup or honey (for babies over 1 year)

Mix the oats, sultanas and apple and mango juice in a bowl, cover and leave to soak overnight in the fridge. In the morning stir in the remaining ingredients and any extra fruit and drizzle over a little maple syrup or honey (if using).

Banana and Prune Fool

This only takes a couple of minutes to prepare and it is very tasty. It is also a good recipe to try if your baby is a little bit constipated.

MAKES 1 PORTION

5 canned prunes in fruit juice, stoned
1 small ripe banana, peeled

1 tablespoon natural yoghurt
1 tablespoon cream cheese

Whiz the prunes, banana, yoghurt and cream cheese together in a blender with 1–2 tablespoons of the juice from the canned fruit.

The Three Bears' Breakfast

This makes a very nutritious breakfast, but make sure your child gobbles it up before Goldilocks comes to the front door!

MAKES 2 ADULT PORTIONS

300 ml/10 fl oz milk
40 g/1½ oz porridge oats

25 g/1 oz ready-to-eat dried peaches or apricots, chopped
1 teaspoon chopped raisins

Pour the milk into a saucepan and bring to the boil. Mix in the oats and bring back to the boil, stirring. Add the chopped dried fruit, lower the heat and simmer for about 4 minutes or until thickened.

Matzo Brei

For those of you who have never heard of matzo, it is a large square of unleavened bread similar to crispbread. When uncooked, it is very brittle and Nicholas loved to snap it into pieces and strew it all over the floor. This is why I prefer to serve it cooked!

MAKES 2 ADULT PORTIONS

2 matzos
1 egg, beaten

25 g/1 oz butter
a little caster sugar (optional)

Break the matzos into bite-sized pieces and soak for a couple of minutes in cold water. Squeeze out the excess water, then add the matzos to the beaten egg. Melt the butter in a frying pan until sizzling and fry the matzos on both sides. Sprinkle with sugar if wished.

French Toast Cut-Outs

It's fun sometimes to cut the bread into a variety of animal shapes using biscuit cutters. For a treat, serve with maple syrup or jam.

MAKES 2 PORTIONS

1 egg
2 tablespoons milk
a pinch of ground cinnamon (optional)

2 slices white or raisin bread
25 g / 1 oz butter

Beat the egg lightly with the milk and cinnamon, if using, and pour into a shallow dish. Dip the bread in this mixture, coating each side. Melt the butter and fry the slices or animal shapes until golden on both sides.

Cheese Scramble

Until your child is one year, scrambled egg should be cooked until it is quite firm and not runny. You could use cottage cheese instead of Cheddar.

MAKES 1 PORTION

1 egg
1 tablespoon milk
15 g / ½ oz butter

1 tablespoon Cheddar cheese, finely grated
1 tomato, skinned and deseeded

Beat the egg with the milk. Melt the butter over a low heat, then add the egg mixture. Cook slowly, stirring all the time. When the mixture has thickened and looks soft and creamily set, add the cheese and chopped tomato. Serve immediately.

FRUIT

Baked Apples with Raisins

Cooking apples have a better flavour, but eating apples are sweeter. You can use either for this recipe. The apples are delicious served with ice cream or custard.

MAKES 6 BABY OR 2 ADULT PORTIONS

2 apples
120 ml/ 4 fl oz apple juice or water
2 tablespoons raisins
a little ground cinnamon

1 tablespoon honey or maple syrup
(if using cooking apples)
a little butter or margarine

Core the apples and prick the skins with a fork to stop them bursting. Put the apples in an ovenproof dish and pour the apple juice or water around the base. Put 1 tablespoon of the raisins into the centre of each apple, sprinkle with cinnamon and (if using cooking apples) pour over honey or maple syrup. Top each with a little butter. Bake in an oven pre-heated to 180°C/350°F/Gas 4 for about 45 minutes.

For young babies, scoop out the pulp of the apple and purée roughly with the raisins and some of the juices from the dish.

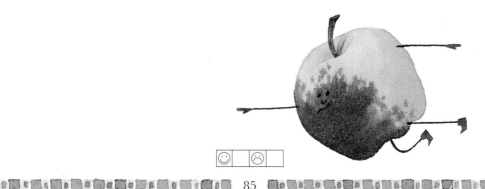

Apple and Blackberry

Blackberries and apples make a delicious combination, and the blackberries (which are rich in Vitamin C) turn the apples a wonderful purple colour. Instead of blackberries you could use other berry fruits like strawberries or blueberries, or a mixture.

MAKES 6 PORTIONS

2 cooking apples, peeled, cored and chopped

100 g/4 oz blackberries
50 g/2 oz soft brown sugar

Cook the apples and blackberries in a saucepan with the sugar and 2 tablespoons water. Cook until the apples are soft (15–20 minutes). Put the fruit through a mouli to make into a smooth purée.

Rice Pudding with Peaches

MAKES 6 PORTIONS

15 g/½ oz butter
50 g/2 oz pudding rice
1 tablespoon each vanilla and caster sugars, or 2 tablespoons caster sugar
600 ml/1 pint milk

1 teaspoon vanilla essence
1 heaped tablespoon raisins
100 ml/3½ fl oz peach juice
2 ripe peaches, skinned, stoned and cut into pieces

Grease a shallow ovenproof dish with a little butter (a 1-litre/1¾-pint oval Pyrex dish is ideal). Put the rice, sugar, milk and vanilla essence into the dish and stir well. Dot with the remaining butter. Bake in an oven preheated to 150°C/300°F/Gas 2 for about 2 hours, stirring after 30 minutes and again 30 minutes later. Meanwhile, simmer the raisins in the peach juice and purée the peaches. When the rice pudding is cooked, stir in the peach juice, raisins and peach purée.

Fresh Pear with Semolina

This recipe is also good with apricots or apple purée with cinnamon. If you do not have any semolina, you can add a finely crushed rusk to the milk (which does not need to be boiled).

MAKES 2 PORTIONS

1 tablespoon semolina
120 ml / 4 fl oz milk
1 ripe pear, peeled, cored and sliced

2 teaspoons maple syrup
a pinch of ground cinnamon

Put the semolina and milk in a saucepan, bring to the boil and simmer for 2 minutes. Add the pear, maple syrup and cinnamon, then put all the ingredients through a mouli to make a purée or chop the pear finely.

Strawberry Rice Pudding

The secret of a good rice pudding is long, slow, gentle cooking. It is good mixed with fruit purée like stewed apples and pears, stewed plums, or chopped canned peaches or apricots.

MAKES 6 BABY OR 3 ADULT PORTIONS

15 g / ½ oz butter
50 g / 2 oz pudding rice
1–2 tablespoons caster sugar

600 ml / 1 pint milk
½ teaspoon vanilla essence
strawberry jam or golden syrup to taste

Grease a shallow ovenproof dish with a little butter. Put the rice and sugar into the dish, pour over the milk and vanilla essence and dot with a little butter. Bake in an oven preheated to 150°C/300°F/Gas 2 for about 2 hours, stirring occasionally. Serve hot with strawberry jam, golden syrup or fruit purée swirled into the rice.

Cheese and Raisin Delight

This makes a delicious combination and is very nutritious.

MAKES 1 PORTION

25 g/1 oz Gruyère cheese
½ apple, peeled and cored

15 g/½ oz raisins, chopped
1 tablespoon mild natural yoghurt

Grate the Gruyère cheese and apple and mix in the raisins and yoghurt. For young babies who do not chew, put all the ingredients in a blender for about 1 minute.

Dried Apricots with Papaya and Pear

Dried apricots are rich in betacarotene and iron and they combine well with a variety of fresh fruits. This is also good mixed with yoghurt. I found that my children also liked chewing on semi-dried apple rings which are easy to hold because of the hole in the middle.

MAKES 4 PORTIONS

50 g/2 oz ready-to-eat dried apricots
½ ripe papaya, peeled, deseeded and chopped

1 ripe juicy pear, peeled, cored and chopped

Put the apricots into a small saucepan and just cover with water. Bring to the boil and simmer until softened (about 8 minutes). Chop the apricots and mix with the chopped papaya and pear, or purée for babies who prefer a smoother texture.

VEGETABLES
Risotto with Butternut Squash

Cooked rice with vegetables is nice and soft so it's a good way to introduce texture to your baby's food. Butternut squash is now more readily available in supermarkets and it is rich in Vitamin A. You could use pumpkin to make this, instead of squash.

MAKES 4 PORTIONS

50 g/2 oz onion, chopped
25 g/1 oz butter
100 g/4 oz basmati rice
450 ml/16 fl oz boiling water

150 g/5 oz butternut squash, peeled and chopped
3 ripe tomatoes (about 225 g/8 oz), skinned, deseeded and chopped
50 g/2 oz Cheddar cheese, grated

Sauté the onion in half the butter until softened. Stir in the rice until well coated. Pour over the boiling water, cover and cook for 8 minutes over a high heat. Stir in the butternut squash, reduce the heat and cook, covered for about 12 minutes or until the water has been absorbed.

Meanwhile, melt the remaining butter in a small saucepan, add the chopped tomatoes and sauté for 2–3 minutes. Stir in the cheese until melted. Add the tomato and cheese mixture to the cooked rice and combine. Season to taste for babies over one year.

Lentil and Vegetable Purée

This makes a delicious purée which my nine-month-old daughter Lara loved. Lentils are an excellent source of protein and very easy to cook.

MAKES 8 PORTIONS

25 g / 1 oz butter
100 g / 4 oz leek, washed and sliced
175 g / 6 oz carrots, peeled and chopped
50 g / 2 oz split red lentils

350 ml / 12 fl oz vegetable stock (see page 33) or water
100 g / 4 oz cauliflower, broken into florets
½ apple, peeled, cored and chopped

Melt the butter in a saucepan and sauté the leek for about 5 minutes. Add the carrots and continue to cook for 2–3 minutes. Add the lentils, pour over the stock, bring to the boil, then cover and simmer for 10 minutes. Add the cauliflower and apple and continue to cook for about 15 minutes or until the lentils and vegetables are tender. Process in a blender to the desired consistency.

☺ ☹ ❄

Multicoloured Casserole

Babies love the bright colours and miniature size of these vegetables. It makes eating fun, and is a good lesson in finger control.

MAKES 4 PORTIONS

1 tablespoon olive oil
1 shallot, peeled and finely chopped
40 g / 1½ oz red pepper, diced

100 g / 4 oz frozen peas
100 g / 4 oz frozen sweetcorn
120 ml / 4 fl oz vegetable stock or water

Heat the oil in a saucepan, add the shallot and red pepper and cook for 3 minutes. Add the peas and sweetcorn, pour over the vegetable stock and bring to the boil. Cover and simmer for 3–4 minutes.

Cabbage Surprise

This is a delicious recipe and very simple to prepare. It makes a great lunch-time meal for the whole family; just increase the quantities, sprinkle with extra grated cheese, either Cheddar or Parmesan and brown under a preheated grill before serving. Alternatively, after you have mixed all the ingredients together, bake in an oven preheated to 180°C/350°F/Gas 4 for 15 minutes.

MAKES 6 PORTIONS

25 g/1 oz brown rice　　　　*a little margarine or oil*
75 g/3 oz cabbage, shredded　　*50 g/2 oz Cheddar cheese, grated*
1 tomato, skinned, deseeded and chopped

Cook the rice in water until quite soft (about 25 minutes). Steam the cabbage or boil in water until tender. Sauté the tomato in a little margarine or oil, add the well-drained cabbage and continue to cook for a further 2 minutes. Stir in the grated cheese and cook over a low heat until all the cheese has melted. Mix the cabbage, tomato and cheese together with the cooked rice and chop it into small pieces.

Vegetables in Cheese Sauce

MAKES 6 PORTIONS

*100 g/4 oz cauliflower, broken into
florets
1 carrot, peeled and thinly sliced
50 g/2 oz frozen peas
100 g/4 oz courgettes, sliced*

*Cheese Sauce
25 g/1 oz margarine
2 tablespoons plain flour
250 ml/8 fl oz milk
50 g/2 oz Cheddar cheese, grated*

Steam the cauliflower and carrot for 6 minutes, then add the peas and courgettes and cook for a further 4 minutes. For a young baby, cook the vegetables until they are soft.

Meanwhile make the cheese sauce in the usual way (see page 59). Mash, chop or purée the vegetables with the sauce.

Green Fingers

French beans make good finger food and work well with this tasty sauce. Alternatively, chop the beans into short lengths and mix with the sauce.

MAKES 2 PORTIONS

*150 g/5 oz French beans, trimmed
1 small onion, peeled and finely chopped
15 g/½ oz butter*

*2 medium tomatoes (225 g/8 oz),
skinned, deseeded and chopped
½ tablespoon tomato purée
25 g/1 oz Gruyère cheese, grated*

Steam the beans for 6 minutes until tender. Sauté the onion in the butter for 4 minutes, add the tomatoes and tomato purée and cook for 3 minutes. Place the beans in an ovenproof dish, cover with the tomato sauce and sprinkle over the cheese. Place under a preheated grill until the cheese is bubbling and golden.

FISH

A Parcel of Plaice

Easy to make and all the flavour is sealed in a parcel.

MAKES 3 PORTIONS

1 fillet (about 100 g/ 4 oz) plaice, skinned
15 g/½ oz butter, melted
1 medium tomato, skinned, deseeded and chopped

1 small courgette, trimmed and diced
1 dessertspoon fresh chives, snipped
1 sprig of fresh parsley
a squeeze of lemon juice

Place the fish fillet on a piece of greased aluminium foil. Mix all the remaining ingredients together and place on top of the fish. Wrap up securely. Cook in an oven preheated to 180°C/350°F/Gas 4 for about 12 minutes or until the fish just flakes with a fork. Remove the herb sprig and mash with a fork.

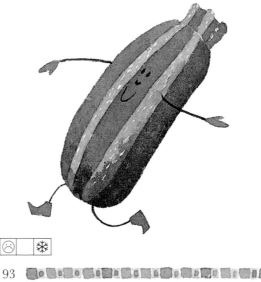

Fingers of Sole

These fingers of sole are fun for babies and toddlers to eat, and make great finger food. They can be served plain or you can dip them into a home-made tomato sauce. Simply purée 3 skinned and deseeded tomatoes with a sautéed shallot, 1 tablespoon tomato purée, 1 dessertspoon of milk and a teaspoon of finely chopped basil.

These 'fish fingers' are much better for your child than commercial ones, which are full of colouring and additives. If you are not using all the fingers at once, it is best to freeze them before they are cooked. You can then take out as many fingers as you need for a freshly cooked meal. Crushed cornflakes also make a delicious coating for other types of fish like haddock or cod.

MAKES 8 PORTIONS

1 shallot, peeled and finely chopped
1 dessertspoon lemon juice
1 tablespoon vegetable oil
1 sole, filleted and skinned
1 egg

1 dessertspoon milk
plain flour
crushed cornflakes
a little butter or margarine for frying

Mix together the chopped shallot, lemon juice and oil. Marinate the fish fillets in this mixture for 1 hour. Remove the fillets from the marinade. Cut them into four or five diagonal strips, depending on the size of the sole. Beat the egg together with the milk. Dip the strips first into the flour, then the egg and milk and finally the crushed cornflakes. Fry the fingers in butter until golden brown on both sides. They should take no more than a few minutes to cook.

Fillets of Sole with Grapes

Fillets of sole with grapes makes a delicious combination. This recipe is quick and easy to prepare and one that the whole family can enjoy.

MAKES 4 ADULT PORTIONS

8 single sole fillets
1 tablespoon seasoned flour
20 g/¾ oz butter
75 g/3 oz button mushrooms, thinly sliced
100 ml/3½ fl oz fish stock

100 ml/3½ fl oz double cream
1 teaspoon lemon juice
2 teaspoons fresh parsley, chopped
20 seedless white grapes, halved
salt and pepper (from one year)

Coat the fish with seasoned flour, melt half the butter in a large frying pan and fry the fish over a medium heat for about 2 minutes on each side until lightly golden. Transfer to a plate and keep warm.

Add the remaining butter to the pan and cook the mushrooms for 3 minutes. Add the stock and simmer for 2 minutes. Stir in the cream and lemon juice and then simmer for 2 minutes. Add the parsley and grapes, then season with salt and pepper (if using) and pour over the fish.

Haddock with Vegetables in a Cheese Sauce

Babies love bright colours, and the yellow of the sweetcorn with the red and green of the tomato and leek makes this dish look attractive. Be careful not to overcook the fish or it will become dry. Once cooked, the fish will just flake with a fork and, mixed with the cheese sauce, will be nice and soft for your baby to eat.

MAKES 6 PORTIONS

175 g/6 oz fillet of haddock, skinned
a little butter
a squeeze of lemon
25 g/1 oz leek, washed and shredded
50 g/2 oz frozen sweetcorn
1 tomato, skinned, deseeded and chopped

Cheese Sauce
15 g/½ oz butter
1 tablespoon plain flour
175 ml/6 fl oz milk
40 g/1½ oz Cheddar cheese, grated

Put the fish into a suitable dish, dot with butter and add a squeeze of lemon juice. Cover with a lid and microwave for 4 minutes on High. Alternatively, cook the fish in an oven preheated to 180°C/350°F/Gas 4 for 8–10 minutes.

Sauté the leek in a knob of butter for 2 minutes. Steam the sweetcorn or cook in boiling water until tender (about 6 minutes). Make the cheese sauce in the usual way (see page 59). Flake the fish with a fork and stir it, the vegetables and tomato into the cheese sauce.

Salmon with a Creamy Chive Sauce

Salmon is easy to cook. It can be cooked very quickly in the microwave but here I have wrapped it in aluminium foil with some vegetables and herbs and cooked it more slowly to bring out the flavour.

MAKES 5 PORTIONS

*100 g/4 oz fillet of salmon or 1 small
salmon cutlet
1 dessertspoon lemon juice
½ small onion, peeled and sliced
½ bay leaf
1 small tomato, cut into chunks
1 sprig of fresh parsley
a little butter*

Chive Sauce
*15 g/½ oz butter
1 tablespoon plain flour
150 ml/5 fl oz milk
cooking liquid from the fish
1 dessertspoon fresh chives, snipped*

Wrap the salmon in aluminium foil with the rest of the ingredients and bake in an oven preheated to 180°C/350°F/Gas 4 for 15 minutes. Meanwhile, make a white sauce, using the butter, flour and milk in the usual way (see page 59).

Once the salmon is cooked, remove it from the foil, strain off the cooking liquid and add this to the white sauce. Finally, stir the chives into the sauce. Flake the salmon and pour the chive sauce over it.

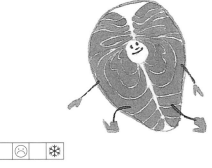

☺ ☹ ❄

CHICKEN

Chicken with Couscous

MAKES 4 PORTIONS

15 g/½ oz butter
25 g/1 oz chopped onion
25 g/1 oz frozen peas (cooked)

175 ml/6 fl oz chicken stock (see page 62)
65 g/2½ oz quick-cooking couscous
50 g/2 oz diced cooked chicken

Melt the butter in a saucepan and sauté the onion until softened but not coloured. Stir in the frozen peas, pour over the stock, bring to the boil and cook for 3 minutes. Stir in the couscous, remove from the heat, cover and set aside for 6 minutes. Fluff the couscous with a fork and mix in the diced chicken.

Chicken and Apple Balls

This is a great favourite with my family. Grated apple adds a delicious flavour to these chicken balls, which makes them appealing to young children and they are delicious hot or cold. These little balls make perfect finger food.

MAKES 20 CHICKEN BALLS

1 large Granny Smith apple, peeled and grated
2 large chicken breasts, cut into chunks
1 onion, finely chopped
½ tablespoon fresh parsley, chopped
1 tablespoon fresh thyme or sage, chopped, or a pinch mixed dried herbs

1 chicken stock cube, crumbled (from one year)
50 g/2 oz fresh white breadcrumbs
salt and freshly ground pepper (from one year)
plain flour for coating
vegetable oil for frying

Using your hands, squeeze out a little excess liquid from the grated apple. Mix the apple with the chicken, onion, herbs, stock cube (from one year) and breadcrumbs and roughly chop in a food processor for a few seconds. Season with a little salt and pepper (from one year).

With your hands, form into about 20 little balls, roll in flour and fry in shallow oil for about 5 minutes until lightly golden and cooked through.

Bang Bang Chicken

So called because my son likes to help when I flatten the chicken by banging it with a mallet! You can prepare these chicken fingers in advance. Before frying, wrap each strip separately and freeze. Just take one or two strips out of the freezer and fry them for freshly cooked chicken fingers.

MAKES 8 PORTIONS

2 chicken breasts, off the bone and skinned
3 slices bread
1½ tablespoons grated Parmesan cheese (optional)

1 tablespoon fresh parsley, chopped (optional)
plain flour for coating
1 egg, beaten
vegetable oil

Cover the chicken with greaseproof paper and flatten with a mallet or rolling pin, then cut each breast lengthways into four strips. Make breadcrumbs from the slices of bread in a food processor. If you are using the Parmesan and parsley, mix these together with the breadcrumbs in a bowl.

Dip the chicken into the flour, then into the egg and then finally into the breadcrumbs. Fry in oil for 3–4 minutes each side until golden on the outside and cooked through. Drain on absorbent kitchen paper and serve.

Chicken with Potato and Swede

A good way to gradually introduce texture is to combine chopped food with creamy mashed potatoes – this can work well with chicken, meat or fish. You could use carrot instead of swede.

MAKES 5 PORTIONS

200 g/7 oz potato, peeled and chopped
200 g/7 oz swede, peeled and chopped
75 g/3 oz chicken, cut into chunks

250 ml/8 fl oz chicken stock (see page 62)
20 g/³⁄₄ oz butter
3 tablespoons milk

Put the potato and swede in a saucepan, pour over some boiling water, then cover and cook over a medium heat for 20 minutes or until the vegetables are tender. Meanwhile, poach the chicken in the stock for 6–8 minutes or until cooked through (allow to cool in the stock).

Drain the swede and potato and mash together with the butter and milk. Chop the chicken into small pieces and mix with the mashed vegetables.

Chicken with Cornflakes

Cornflakes are very versatile and I often use them instead of breadcrumbs to coat both chicken and fish. These strips of chicken make good finger food. Before cooking, they can be individually wrapped and frozen.

MAKES 3–4 PORTIONS

1 egg, beaten
1 tablespoon milk
25 g/1 oz cornflakes, crushed

1 large chicken breast, skinned, off the bone and cut into about 8 strips
15 g/¹⁄₂ oz butter, melted

Mix together the egg and milk in a shallow dish. In a separate dish spread out the cornflake crumbs. Dip the strips of chicken first into the egg and then coat with the cornflakes. Put the chicken strips into a greased ovenproof dish, drizzle over the melted butter and toss to coat. Bake in an oven preheated to 180°C/350°F/Gas 4 for about 10 minutes on each side or until cooked through. Alternatively, the chicken strips can be sautéed in vegetable oil until golden and cooked through.

Chicken with Summer Vegetables

In the summer, you can often find different varieties of squash – some are round, some green and some yellow. They are all delicious, but this recipe can also be made simply with courgettes.

MAKES 6 PORTIONS

1 small onion, chopped
1 garlic clove, crushed
¼ sweet red pepper, deseeded and finely chopped
1½ tablespoons olive oil
1 chicken breast, cut into chunks
2 tablespoons apple juice

175 ml/6 fl oz chicken stock (see page 62)
225 g/8 oz summer squash, chopped, or 1 large/2 small courgettes, finely chopped
200 g/7 oz sweet potato, peeled and chopped
1 tablespoon fresh basil, torn

Sauté the onion, garlic and sweet pepper in the olive oil until softened. Stir in the chicken and continue to cook for 3–4 minutes. Pour over the apple juice and stock and stir in the squash or courgette, sweet potato and basil. Bring to the boil, then cover and simmer for about 10 minutes. Chop or purée to the desired consistency.

Chicken with Winter Vegetables

This is quick and easy to prepare and has a delicious rich chicken flavour.
It is good with mashed potato.

MAKES 6 PORTIONS

2 chicken breasts, on the bone and skinned
a little flour
vegetable oil
1 leek, white part only, washed and sliced

1 small onion, peeled and finely chopped
1 carrot, peeled and sliced
1 celery stalk, trimmed and sliced
300 ml/10 fl oz chicken stock (see page 62)

Cut the chicken breasts in half, roll them in flour and brown them in a little oil for 3–4 minutes. In another frying pan, sauté the leek and onion in a little oil for 5 minutes until soft and golden. Put the chicken into a casserole together with all the vegetables and the stock. Cook in an oven preheated to 180°C/350°F/Gas 4 for 1 hour, stirring halfway through.

Take the chicken off the bone and chop it into little pieces with the vegetables or purée it together with the cooking liquid in a mouli or blender.

RED MEATS

Beef Casserole with Carrots

The secret for a delicious rich taste is to cook the meat for a long time so that it is very tender and has a good flavour from the onions and carrots. Increase the Marmite for toddlers.

MAKES 10 PORTIONS

2 medium onions, peeled and sliced
vegetable oil
350 g / 12 oz lean stewing beef, trimmed and cut into small chunks
2 medium carrots, peeled and sliced

1 beef stock cube, crumbled or 1 teaspoon Marmite (for babies over one year)
1 tablespoon fresh parsley, chopped
600 ml / 1 pint water
2 large potatoes, cut into quarters

Fry the onion until golden in a little oil, then add the meat chunks and brown. Transfer the meat and onions to a small casserole and add all the rest of the ingredients except for the potatoes. Cook, covered, in an oven preheated to 180°C/350°F/Gas 4 for 30 minutes, then turn down the heat and cook for a further 2½ hours at 160°C/325°F/Gas 3. 1 hour before you finish cooking the meat, add the potatoes.

Chop the meat quite finely in a food processor or blender so that it is easy for your baby to chew. If the meat gets too dry whilst cooking, add a little extra water. You can also add mushrooms and tomatoes to this recipe for variation and they should be added 30 minutes before the end of cooking time.

☺ ☹ ❄

Tasty Liver Casserole

Liver is very good for children: it is easy to digest, a good source of iron and is very easy to cook. I must admit that I dislike the taste having been forced to eat liver at school, but, to my great surprise, my one-year-old son adored it. This recipe is good served with mashed potato.

MAKES 4 PORTIONS

100 g/4 oz calf's liver, trimmed and sliced
2 tablespoons vegetable oil
1 small onion, peeled and chopped
1 large or 2 medium carrots (approx.

125 g/4½ oz), peeled and chopped
200 ml/7 fl oz chicken or vegetable stock
2 medium tomatoes (approx. 200 g/7 oz), skinned, deseeded and chopped
1 dessertspoon fresh parsley, chopped

Sauté the liver in 1 tablespoon of the oil until browned, then set aside. Heat the remaining oil in a saucepan and sauté the onion for 2–3 minutes. Add the chopped carrot and sauté for 2 minutes, then pour over the stock, bring to the boil, cover and simmer over a low heat for about 15 minutes. Chop the liver into pieces and add to the pan together with the tomatoes and parsley, and cook for about 3 minutes. You can either serve with mashed potato as it is or blend the mixture for a few seconds to make a rough purée.

Savoury Veal Casserole

A delicious casserole of veal, vegetables and fresh herbs – just increase the quantities for a meal the whole family can enjoy.

MAKES 3 PORTIONS

1 small onion, peeled and finely chopped
1 carrot, scraped and sliced
½ celery stalk, sliced
vegetable oil

100 g/4 oz lean veal for stewing
1 sprig of fresh rosemary
1 sprig of fresh parsley
120 ml/4 fl oz water

Fry the onion, carrot and celery in a little oil for 3 minutes. Cut the veal into chunks and put it into a saucepan with the vegetables, herbs and the water. Simmer slowly, covered for 1 hour (stirring once). Remove the herbs and roughly chop the veal and vegetables in a food processor.

Special Steak

This recipe makes a very good introduction to red meat for your baby.

MAKES 4 PORTIONS

1 potato (about 225 g / 8 oz), peeled and chopped
1 shallot or 25 g / 1 oz onion, peeled and finely chopped
1 tablespoon vegetable oil
100 g / 4 oz fillet steak

50 g / 2 oz button mushrooms, washed and chopped
15 g / ½ oz butter
1 tomato, skinned, deseeded and chopped
2 tablespoons milk

Boil the potato until tender, then drain. Meanwhile, sauté the shallot in the vegetable oil until softened. Spoon half the shallots on to a piece of aluminium foil. Cut the steak into slices 1 cm / ½ inch thick and place on top of the shallots. Spread the remaining shallots over the steak. Cook under a preheated grill for 3 minutes each side or until cooked. Sauté the button mushrooms in half of the butter for 2 minutes, add the chopped tomato and continue to cook for 1 minute. Mash the potato with the milk and the remaining butter until smooth. Chop or purée the steak together with the shallots, mushrooms and tomato and mix with the mashed potato.

Mini Shepherd's Pie

Shepherd's pie was always a great 'comfort food' on a winter's evening when I was a child. Try making small portions in ramekin dishes for your child. See page 155 for a more grown-up version.

MAKES 2–4 PORTIONS

200 g/7 oz potatoes, peeled and chopped
100 g/4 oz carrot, peeled and chopped
1 tablespoon olive oil
small onion, peeled and chopped
1 small garlic clove, peeled and crushed
25 g/1 oz red pepper, cored, deseeded and diced

150 g/5 oz lean minced beef
1 tablespoon fresh parsley, chopped
1 teaspoon tomato purée
100 ml/3½ fl oz chicken stock (see page 62)
a generous knob of butter
1 tablespoon milk

Put the potato and carrot into a saucepan, cover with boiling water and cook until the vegetables are tender (about 20 minutes).

Meanwhile heat the oil in a frying pan and sauté the onion, garlic and red pepper for 2–3 minutes. Add the minced beef and sauté until browned. At this stage it is a good idea to chop the meat in a food processor for a few seconds to give it a smoother texture. Return to the pan, add the parsley, tomato purée and chicken stock, bring to the boil, then cover and simmer for about 15 minutes.

When the potato and carrot are cooked, drain and mash together with some of the butter and the milk until smooth. Mix with the meat and spoon into small (10 cm/4 inch) ramekin dishes. Heat through in an oven preheated to 180°C/350°F/Gas 4, then dot with the remaining butter and place under a preheated grill until lightly golden.

Tasty Rice with Meat and Vegetables

MAKES 8 PORTIONS

½ onion, peeled and finely chopped
1 carrot, scrubbed and finely chopped
1 tablespoon vegetable oil
225 g/8 oz lean minced beef
400 g/14 oz canned chopped tomatoes
a few drops of Worcestershire sauce

Rice
50 g/2 oz basmati rice
300 ml/10 fl oz chicken stock (see page 62)
½ small sweet red pepper, deseeded and finely chopped
50 g/2 oz frozen peas

Rinse the rice and place in a saucepan with the chicken stock. Bring to the boil, then cover and simmer for 10 minutes. Add the red pepper and peas and cook, uncovered, for 6–7 minutes, or until the rice is tender and there is no liquid left.

Meanwhile sauté the onion and carrot in the vegetable oil for 5 minutes. Add the minced meat and cook, stirring, until browned. Transfer the meat into a food processor and chop for 30 seconds to make it easier for your baby to chew. Return the meat to the pan and add the tomatoes and Worcestershire sauce. Cook over a low heat for 10 minutes. Stir in the rice and cook for 3–4 minutes.

PASTA

Salmon and Broccoli Tagliatelle

Pasta is popular with babies and toddlers so combining it with nutritious foods like salmon and broccoli is a good idea.

MAKES 6 PORTIONS

175 g/6 oz tagliatelle
75 g/3 oz broccoli, cut into small florets
300 ml/10 fl oz milk
1 bay leaf
3 peppercorns

a sprig of fresh parsley
150 g/5 oz fillet of salmon, skinned
15 g/½ oz butter
15 g/½ oz flour
½ teaspoon lemon juice
50 g/2 oz grated Cheddar cheese

Cook the tagliatelle according to the packet instructions. Steam the broccoli or cook in boiling water for about 4 minutes or until tender.

Pour the milk into a saucepan together with the bay leaf, peppercorns and parsley and bring to the boil. Reduce the heat, place the salmon in the pan and simmer covered for 6–8 minutes or until the fish is just cooked. Remove the salmon with a slotted spoon and strain the milk.

Melt the butter, stir in the flour and cook for 1 minute. Gradually whisk in the reserved milk.Bring to the boil and then simmer for 2 minutes. Stir in the lemon juice and cheese until melted.

Flake the fish and stir into the cheese sauce together with the broccoli cut into small pieces. Chop the tagliatelle into short lengths and mix with the cheese sauce.

Bolognese Sauce with Aubergine

MAKES 12 PORTIONS OF SAUCE

1 aubergine, peeled and sliced
a little salt
1 medium onion, peeled and chopped
¼ garlic clove, peeled and chopped
vegetable oil for frying
450 g / 1 lb lean minced beef or lamb

2 tablespoons tomato purée
4 tomatoes, skinned, deseeded and chopped
¼ teaspoon mixed dried herbs
2 tablespoons plain flour
450 ml / 16 fl oz chicken stock (see page 62)
100 g / 4 oz mushrooms, washed and sliced

Sprinkle the aubergine with salt and drain for 30 minutes. Rinse and pat dry. Sauté the onion and garlic in oil until soft. Add the meat and cook until browned. Chop in a food processor. Return to the pan, add the tomato purée, tomatoes, herbs, flour and stock. Bring to the boil and simmer for 45 minutes. Fry the aubergine in oil until golden. Pat dry with kitchen paper. Chop in a food processor. Sauté the mushrooms in oil and add to the sauce with the aubergine.

Creamy Chicken Pasta Sauce

MAKES 3 PORTIONS OF SAUCE

1 small chicken breast, off the bone,
skinned and cut into chunks
a little oil or chicken stock, for cooking
40 g / 1½ oz broccoli, broken into florets

15 g / ½ oz butter
1 tablespoon flour
175 ml / 6 fl oz milk
25 g / 1 oz Cheddar cheese, grated

Sauté the chicken or poach in stock until cooked. Steam the broccoli until tender. Melt the butter and stir in the flour. Gradually stir in the milk over a low heat until thickened. Simmer for 1 minute, stirring. Off the heat, stir in the cheese. Mix in the chicken and broccoli, chop or purée and mix with cooked pasta.

Pasta Stars with Tomato and Cheese

This fresh tomato sauce is very tasty and, because it has vegetables and cheese blended into it, it is more nutritious than an ordinary tomato sauce.

MAKES 2 PORTIONS

1 medium carrot peeled and sliced
100 g/4 oz cauliflower florets
3 tablespoons pasta stars or other tiny pasta shapes

25 g/1 oz butter
300 g/11 oz ripe tomatoes, skinned, deseeded and chopped
50 g/2 oz grated Cheddar cheese

Put the sliced carrot into the bottom of a steamer. Cover with boiling water and cook over a medium heat for 10 minutes. Put the cauliflower florets in the steamer basket, place over the carrots, cover and cook for 5 minutes or until the vegetables are tender. Cook the pasta stars in boiling water according to the packet instructions. Meanwhile, melt the butter and sauté the tomatoes for about 3 minutes or until mushy. Stir in the Cheddar cheese until melted. Blend the cooked carrots and cauliflower together with the tomatoes and cheese. Mix with the pasta stars.

Pasta Shells with Tuna and Sweetcorn

Tuna is a good store cupboard standby. It is rich in protein, Vitamin D and Vitamin B12.

MAKES 3 PORTIONS

25 g/1 oz small pasta shells or other small pasta shapes
25 g/1 oz butter
2 tablespoons flour
300 ml/10 fl oz milk

40 g/1½ oz grated Gruyère cheese
1 x 100 g/4 oz canned tuna, drained and flaked
75 g/3 oz canned or cooked frozen sweetcorn

Cook the pasta according to the packet instructions. Melt the butter in a saucepan. Add the flour and stir in for about 1 minute. Slowly add the milk, stirring continuously until the sauce has thickened. Stir in the cheese, tuna, sweetcorn and pasta and heat through.

Tuna Salad

Oily fish like tuna and salmon contain omega-3 fatty acids, which help prevent heart disease and are important for brain and visual development. Unfortunately, fatty acids are destroyed in the canning process of tuna but you could make this salad using fresh tuna or salmon instead.

MAKES 4 PORTIONS

75 g/3 oz cooked pasta bows or shells
1 spring onion, finely chopped, or
1 small shallot, peeled and diced
100 g/4 oz canned tuna in oil, drained
and flaked
3 cherry tomatoes, quartered
25 g/1 oz canned sweetcorn (or cooked
frozen sweetcorn)
1 small avocado, peeled, stoned and cut
into small pieces (optional)

Dressing
1 tablespoon mayonnaise
1 tablespoon olive oil
1 teaspoon fresh lemon juice

Mix together the ingredients for the dressing. Combine the cooked pasta with the salad ingredients and toss with the dressing. If you wish, toast some sesame seeds in a dry frying pan until golden and sprinkle these on top (see page 138).

NINE TO TWELVE MONTH MEAL PLANNER

	Breakfast	Mid-morning	Lunch
Day 1	**Fruity Swiss Muesli** **Dried Apricots with Papaya and** **Pear** served with yoghurt Milk	Milk	**Chicken and Apple Balls** Finger vegetables **Strawberry Rice Pudding** Water
Day 2	Weetabix Cheese on toast Fruit Milk	Milk	**Special Steak** **Home-Made Fruit Jelly** Fruit Water
Day 3	Scrambled egg with toast Fruit with cottage cheese Milk	Milk	**Pasta Shells with Tuna** **and Sweetcorn** Water
Day 4	**My Favourite Pancakes** Fruit Milk	Milk	**Tasty Liver Casserole** **Multicoloured Casserole** Papaya purée Water
Day 5	**French Toast Cut-Outs** **Apricot, Apple and Pear Custard** Milk	Milk	**Bang Bang Chicken** **Cabbage Surprise** **Home-Made Fruit Jelly** Fruit Water
Day 6	**Summer Fruit Muesli** Yoghurt with dried fruit Milk	Milk	**Beef Casserole with Carrot** **Going Bananas** Water
Day 7	**Cheese Scramble** Toast Fingers **Fruity Yoghurt** Milk	Milk	**Chicken with Couscous** **Fresh Pear with Semolina** Water

Mid-afternoon	Dinner	Bedtime
Milk	Finger sandwiches Finger vegetables Juice or water	Milk
Milk	**Pasta Stars with Tomato and Cheese** Fromage frais/Yoghurt Juice or water	Milk
Milk	**Courgette and Pea Souper** Fruit Juice or water	Milk
Milk	**Vegetables in Cheese Sauce** **Apple and Blackberry** Juice or water	Milk
Milk	**Tomato and Courgette Pasta Stars** Fruit Juice or water	Milk
Milk	**Fingers of Sole** Finger vegetables **Rice Pudding with Peaches** Juice or water	Milk
Milk	**Lentil and Vegetable Purée** Sticks of cheese **Baked Apples with Raisins** Juice or water	Milk

CHAPTER FIVE

TODDLERS

I find that, beyond the age of one, toddlers prefer to exercise their independence and feed themselves. The more your toddler experiments using a spoon and fork, the quicker he will master the art of feeding himself – you never know, some food might find its way into his mouth! A 'pelican' bib – a strong plastic bib which has a tray at the bottom to catch stray food – is also good. If your toddler has difficulty eating with a spoon, try giving him finger foods like goujons of fish or raw vegetables with a dip. You must still be careful, though, to keep food like olives, nuts or fresh lychees out of the reach of young children. Toddlers love to put everything in their mouths and it would be so easy for them to choke on such foods.

ENJOYING MEALTIMES TOGETHER

Toddlers only have small tummies and often can't eat enough at mealtimes to fuel their high energy requirements, so they should be offered three meals and three snacks at regular times. There is a whole section in this book on healthy snacks, so don't make the mistake of giving your toddler sweets or processed snacks when he could enjoy eating a dip with a bowl of raw vegetables much more. Toddlers who get used to eating healthy snacks are more likely to continue the same habits later on in life. However, it would also be wrong to make sweets and doughnuts the forbidden fruit, as your toddler would crave them all the more and gorge himself on them whenever he could.

Many toddlers enjoy eating much more sophisticated food than we would imagine possible. Let your child try food from your plate and you may be very surprised by the tastes he enjoys. Of course, food from Mummy's or Daddy's plate is much more interesting than his own meal and you can sometimes entice your child to eat if you put his meal on your plate. But the point at this stage is that the toddler can now eat, to a large extent, what you adults are eating. I am a great believer in giving toddlers 'grown-up' foods as soon as possible and almost all the recipes that follow are suitable for the whole family. *Do* eat with your child rather than just sitting there shovelling food into his mouth. He'll eat much more happily *with* you – after all, who enjoys eating alone?

Try and reform your own eating habits by adding less salt and sugar to your food and your toddler will be able to enjoy almost everything you cook. So, I hope that you will enjoy many happy mealtimes together and that your children will introduce you to some great new recipes!

MY CHILD WON'T EAT!

After the age of one, your child will be expending much more energy and nearly all toddlers at some stage will lose interest in food and would much rather play with their toys and run around. This can be a very difficult time and it is important not to make a big fuss if your child refuses to eat. He will eat when he is hungry and, the more you fuss, the more he will refuse his food. Be patient with him – he will grow out of this phase.

If your toddler really enjoys his food and eats well at mealtimes, then you really are a lucky mother. I know so many mothers who worry constantly that their child is not eating enough. Most of these worries are unnecessary and toddlers can thrive very well on remarkably little food.

Toddlers are very unpredictable: some days they will be ravenous, and other days they will eat practically nothing. If you judge a child's food intake over a whole week, you won't worry as much if one day he refuses to eat anything.

Many mothers complain that their toddler will not touch meat or fish, but there are lots of other equally good sources of protein like peanut butter, eggs or dairy produce. Then there are the mothers who are tearing their hair out because their children will only eat one thing. This is also quite normal: children, unlike adults, like repetition in their diet and they are often wary of trying new foods.

Avoid the empty calories found in biscuits, cakes and sweets and, instead, offer healthy alternatives like fruit or raw vegetables such as carrot and cucumber with a tasty dip or cheese. Don't give drinks just before a meal as this can spoil your baby's appetite.

Unfortunately, over the past 50 years children's consumption of biscuits has risen fourfold, confectionery by 25 times and soft drinks by 34 times. Meanwhile, the consumption of milk, bread, fruit and vegetables has declined. The processed foods and ready meals that are now popular are high in saturated fat, salt and sugar. It is very important to make sure that children eat as much fresh food as possible. One in four children in the UK is overweight and the number of obese children has doubled in the last 20 years.

By this age your child is probably quite independent and may well prefer to feed himself. Toddlers enjoy playing with their food; it's all part of the learning process. Let your toddler eat spaghetti with his hands and poke his finger into the jelly to see it wobble – there is plenty of time to teach him table manners once he has finished experimenting. Let your child help prepare meals – this may well stimulate an interest in food. My son is always willing to lend a helping hand, especially when it comes to making biscuits. He loves to knead the dough, roll it out and cut it into shapes. He thinks it's more fun than play dough !

A great deal of problem eating can be overcome by attractive presentation. Choose foods that are naturally brightly coloured. It is a good idea to use plastic plates with separate compartments and present your toddler with two or three foods in separate sections. We have little Chinese meals at home and you can buy plastic chopsticks that are joined at the top, which even a three-year-old can use. You should see how they enjoy picking the food up with their chopsticks and how wide they open their mouths !

Sometimes it is fun to arrange food in a pattern on the plate. You can help teach your child by arranging food in the shape of numbers or letters or make the food into the shape of a face. You can use some small-sized novelty biscuit cutters to cut out shapes from bread, sandwiches or cheese to stimulate your child's interest. Another tip is to call food by funny names like Peter Rabbit carrots or Noddy soup. You may laugh, but if your toddler thinks this is what his favourite character eats for lunch, he is more likely to eat it himself!

Never put too much food on a plate – much better that he should ask for more. Toddlers love individual portions of food. Make a miniature shepherd's pie (see page 155), for example (much nicer than a dollop of meat and potatoes on a plate) and miniature cakes rather than slices from a large cake.

If you have given your toddler a good choice of foods and he still refuses to eat, it is not, then, a good idea to offer him the contents of the fridge and larder. Explain that this is his meal and that there is nothing

else on offer. If he is very restless and clearly not interested, just put the food back in the fridge and bring it out a little later. You will be making a rod for your own back otherwise, and nine times out of ten he is just not hungry – no child has ever starved to death through stubbornness.

For breakfast, give your child porridge or Weetabix rather than sugar-coated cereals and offer toast with peanut butter or Marmite rather than toast and jam. Cheese on toast and well-cooked scrambled

eggs are other healthy breakfast options. For supper, chicken on the griddle is a good alternative to chicken nuggets, give fish pie rather than fish fingers, pasta with broccoli or home-made tomato sauce rather than spaghetti hoops, mini minute steaks instead of frozen burgers, and shepherd's pie instead of sausages and chips. For snacks, give popcorn instead of crisps, and dried fruit like apricots or yoghurt-covered raisins instead of sweets. Give juice or smoothies that are 100 per cent fruit juice instead of fruit juice drinks which often contain less than 10 per cent juice and lots of sugar and water.

If you make eating fun, then your child will enjoy tucking in with you. An occasional trip to a restaurant does wonders to stimulate a child's appetite. Even just going to a friend's house for tea can help sometimes, especially if there is another child present who likes to tuck in!

THE FOODS TO CHOOSE
Children under five need more dietary fat than adults in proportion to their body weight so unless your child is overweight, don't give him foods that are low fat. Fat is a rich source of energy and fat-soluble vitamins which your toddler needs in order to grow. There are, of course, exceptions to the rule, and an overweight toddler should have his fat intake restricted by cutting down on processed and fatty foods and switching to low-fat dairy products.

High-fibre foods in large amounts are also unsuitable as they are bulky and filling and do not supply enough calories for a rapidly growing toddler. Also, a high-fibre diet can hinder the absorption of vital minerals like iron. Provided your child eats plenty of fruit and vegetables he will get all the fibre he needs.

Once your child is twelve months old you can switch from formula to whole cow's milk, but don't give semi-skimmed milk before the age of two as it is low in energy, which your child needs to grow. Skimmed milk should not be introduced before five years. Children over one year need 400 ml/14 fl oz of whole milk a day. For children who are very picky, there may be advantages to continuing with a follow-on formula (which is fortified with vitamins and iron) until two years of age.

Although more and more people seem to be turning away from red meat in favour of fish and chicken, bear in mind that red meat provides more iron and zinc than either fish or poultry. Try making tasty meals with lean minced meat – a good tip is to cook the meat and then chop it in a food processor so that it is not lumpy, and there are some lovely recipes for Beefburgers, Meatballs and Shepherd's Pie (see pages 153–55) that make excellent family meals.

Try to avoid processed meats like sausages, salami and corned beef.

If you are bringing your child up on a vegetarian diet or if he simply dislikes eating meat, make sure that you include nutrient-dense foods like cheese and eggs in his diet. Provided your toddler is eating a good variety of food types, a vegetarian diet can provide all the nutrients he needs. It is very important to include vegetarian sources of iron such as green vegetables, pulses, fortified breakfast cereals and dried fruit every day, and make sure you give foods or drinks containing Vitamin C at the same meal as this helps to boost the iron in non-meat sources.

Pasta remains a great favourite with toddlers and you can combine it with other healthy foods such as vegetables and

tuna. Individual pieces of pasta like penne or fusilli tend to be easiest for toddlers to eat. (Although, when my son, Nicholas, was 20 months old he invented his own method of eating spaghetti – he held it out in front of him by the two ends and sucked in from the middle! Not the height of good manners perhaps, but certainly very efficient.)

Fruit and Desserts

There are many recipes in this chapter for delicious hot and cold desserts that are easy to prepare and can be enjoyed by the whole family. However, there is still nothing more delicious or better for you than fresh ripe fruit, so make sure your child has plenty of it every day. None of the vitamins or nutrients are destroyed through cooking, and fruit makes great finger food for your toddler.

Fruits are packed with powerful antioxidants and natural compounds called phytochemicals, which help boost immunity and protect the body from heart disease and cancer. The incidence of cancer is increasing. Approximately one third of cancer cases are related to what we eat and researchers estimate that a diet filled with fruit and vegetables instead of fats and processed foods, along with exercise, could reduce the incidence of cancer by at least 30 per cent.

Whole fruit in a fruit bowl isn't that appealing to a hungry child, but if you have a selection of fresh fruit cut up and placed on a low shelf in the fridge, this will help stop your child from snacking on crisps or chocolate biscuits.

Dried fruits, especially apricots, are very nutritious as the drying process concentrates the nutrients. However, take care not to give dried fruit too often in between meals, as they stick to the teeth and even natural sugars cause tooth decay.

Kiwi fruit and citrus and berry fruits are rich in Vitamin C, which helps to boost iron absorption, so try to make sure you include these in your child's diet. You can add fresh or dried fruits to breakfast cereals. It's also a good idea to buy a juicer so you can make your own fresh-fruit smoothies. Pure fruit juice and smoothies are also good, but be wary of fruit juice drinks as they often contain as little as 10 per cent juice so always read the label. Juices are a good source of vitamins but remember that only by eating the whole fruit will your child be getting fibre.

As different fruits provide different nutrients, include as much variety as possible in your child's diet. Try introducing

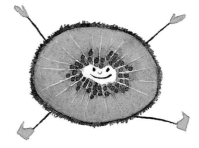

him to some more exotic fruits. One kiwi fruit contains more than the daily adult requirement of Vitamin C and makes a good snack when cut in half, placed in an egg cup and eaten with a teaspoon. You could also make a tropical fruit salad with mango, melon balls, pineapple and a sauce made with fresh orange juice and passion fruit.

You can make delicious and healthy ice-lollies from puréed fresh fruits, yoghurt, fruit juices or smoothies. Ice-lolly moulds are cheap to buy, and one food that almost no child can resist is an ice-lolly so this is a good way to encourage children to eat more fruit.

Ice creams in all colours, shapes and sizes are sold all over the world. However, the quality of some products is put to shame by the genuine, home-made experience. If you do buy ice creams choose those that are made from natural ingredients only. If you want to try your hand at making your own, it really is worth investing in an ice-cream-making machine, which churns the mixture as it freezes. Believe me, you will put it to good use over the years and your children will be very popular with their friends when they come round for tea.

Baking for Toddlers

A toddler's first birthday is a big occasion in his life and probably even more exciting for his parents and grandparents! It is great fun preparing the food for a child's party. Anyone can go to a shop and order a birthday cake in the shape of a train, but how much more impressive and satisfying it is to bake and decorate your own. Your child will love to help with the mixing and decorating – probably more fun than eating it.

Any basic sponge or fruit-cake mixture could be adapted to a novelty shape, if you like. There are many smaller cakes that can be served at a child's tea party. Many of the baking recipes contain healthy ingredients, cutting out undesirables as much as possible, but some are sheer uncompromised treats.

Healthy Snacks

If your toddler is happy to eat three main meals a day, then that is wonderful and very convenient for everyone, but – let's face it – nearly all toddlers snack between meals. Whereas for some this just supplements their main meals, many toddlers do not have the patience to sit down and eat a proper meal and they get most of their nutrition from snacks during the day. Toddlers' stomachs are small and it is often difficult for them to eat enough at breakfast, say, to last them until lunchtime when they have been rushing around all morning. As I said earlier, lots of small meals – healthy snacks – during the day are in fact healthier than three main meals. Snacks are therefore a very important part of a toddler's diet. If you encourage your child when he is very young to enjoy eating healthy snacks in preference to sweets and crisps, it is likely that he will continue these habits later in life and enjoy a much healthier diet.

Keep your larder and fridge full of healthy snacks (see pages 180–81) and, when you take your toddler out, try to remember to take a small bag of healthy snacks with you. Toddlers expend a lot of energy and it doesn't take them long to get hungry again after a meal.

TEXTURES AND QUANTITIES

There is no longer any need to purée your child's food; on the contrary, he should be getting used to chewing. The longer you continue with purées because that is the way your child prefers his food, the more difficult it will become to encourage him to chew and swallow his food properly. In fact chewing on something hard, such as a raw carrot, should help to relieve sore gums. A lot of toddlers, however, do not like to chew chunks of meat, and it is sometimes necessary to break meat down in a blender before serving it. I find that minced meat, liver or chicken tends to go down better with most toddlers than chunks of meat.

With each recipe in this chapter, I have given quantities in adult portions. Every child is different, and you must gauge the portion size on your toddler's appetite. He can eat anything from a quarter of an adult portion to a whole portion if he is exceptionally hungry and greedy!

OVERWEIGHT TODDLERS

In the UK, more than one in five children under the age of four is overweight, and one in ten six-year-olds is obese. If your child is overweight, then you should discuss with your doctor the best ways of decreasing his calorie intake. Adopt a healthier eating plan rather than cutting down on the amount of food offered. No child should ever go hungry. Cut out sugary, fatty and processed foods and give more fresh fruit and vegetables. Give high-fibre cereals like Weetabix or Bran Flakes, give jacket potatoes instead of chips, and grilled or roast chicken instead of chicken nuggets. Semi-skimmed milk can be introduced from two years.

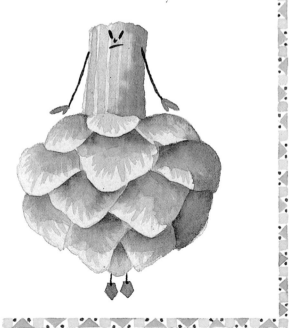

VEGETABLES
Ratatouille with Rice or Pasta

Vegetables tend to be quite soft in ratatouille and so are easy for your toddler to chew. Choose a firm aubergine and courgette; if they are not fresh, the ratatouille may taste bitter. Serve as an accompaniment to a meal with rice, as below, or with pasta shapes. It is suitable for freezing without the rice.

MAKES 4 ADULT PORTIONS

2 tablespoons olive oil
1 red onion, peeled and chopped
1 garlic clove, peeled and crushed
1 small sweet red pepper and 1 small
sweet green pepper, deseeded and diced
1 courgette, trimmed and diced
1 small aubergine, trimmed and diced
400 g/14 oz canned chopped tomatoes

pinch of sugar
1 teaspoon red wine vinegar
salt and pepper

Rice
1 vegetable stock cube
1 bay leaf
200 g/7 oz long-grain rice

Heat the oil in a large saucepan and cook the onion and garlic for 1–2 minutes. Add the peppers and courgette and cook for 4–5 minutes. Add the aubergine and cook for 5 minutes. Stir in the chopped tomatoes, sugar and red wine vinegar, bring to a simmer and then cook for 10 minutes. Season with salt and pepper.

For the rice, place the vegetables, crumbled stock cube and bay leaf in a large saucepan of water. Stir in the rice and cook according to the packet instructions.

Special Fried Rice

Babies love rice and this is very appealing as it is so colourful. For older children you can make little sailing boats. Cut a cooked red pepper in half, stuff each half with rice and stick two corn chips upright in the rice to look like sails.

MAKES 6 ADULT PORTIONS

225 g / 8 oz basmati rice
75 g / 3 oz carrots, scrubbed and diced
75 g / 3 oz frozen peas
75 g / 3 oz sweet red pepper, deseeded and diced

3 tablespoons vegetable oil or vegetable oil with a teaspoon of sesame oil
2 eggs, lightly beaten
1 small onion, peeled and finely chopped
1 spring onion, finely sliced
1 tablespoon soy sauce

Wash the rice thoroughly and cook according to the packet instructions in a saucepan of lightly salted water until tender. Steam the carrot, peas and pepper for 5 minutes or until tender. Heat 1 tablespoon of the oil in a frying pan. Season the eggs with a little salt, add to the pan, tilting it so the eggs form a thin layer over the bottom, and fry until set like a very thin omelette. Remove from the pan and cut into thin strips. Meanwhile, put 2 tablespoons of oil into a wok or frying pan and sauté the chopped onion until softened. Add the steamed vegetables and rice and cook, stirring, for 2–3 minutes. Add the egg and spring onion and cook, stirring, for 2 minutes more. Sprinkle with the soy sauce before serving.

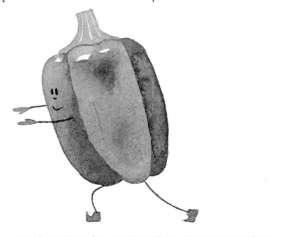

☺ ☹

Stuffed Potatoes

Stuffed potatoes make an excellent meal for toddlers and there are endless variations on the fillings you can make. Prick medium potatoes all over and brush with oil. Bake in an oven preheated to 190°C/375°F/Gas 5 for 1¼–1½ hours or until tender. Alternatively, to speed up the cooking, prick the potatoes, wrap them in absorbent kitchen paper and put them in the microwave on high for 7–8 minutes. Brush the potatoes with oil and then transfer to the oven and cook for about 45–50 minutes or until tender.

Carefully spoon the soft flesh out of the skins, leaving enough round the sides for the skins to keep their shape. You are now ready to make the various fillings.

Vegetable and Cheese Potato Filling

MAKES 4 ADULT PORTIONS

25 g/1 oz each broccoli and cauliflower, broken into small florets
4 medium or 2 large baked potatoes
15 g/½ oz butter
120 ml/4 fl oz milk

50 g/2 oz Cheddar cheese, grated
2 medium tomatoes, skinned and cut into small pieces
½ teaspoon salt
Cheddar cheese, grated, to finish

Steam the broccoli and cauliflower until they are tender (about 6 minutes), then chop finely. Meanwhile, mash the potato flesh with the butter and milk until smooth and creamy. Mix in the cheese, tomatoes, cooked chopped vegetables and salt, and scoop the mixture back into the potato skins. Sprinkle a little extra grated cheese on top and brown under a preheated grill.

Tuna and Sweetcorn Stuffed Potato

If you don't have time to oven-bake the potatoes you can bake them in a
microwave, although they won't have crispy skins.

MAKES 2 ADULT PORTIONS

2 medium baked potatoes
200 g / 7 oz canned tuna in oil, drained
75 g / 3 oz canned or cooked frozen
sweetcorn
2 tablespoons mayonnaise

2 tablespoons milk
2 spring onions, finely sliced (optional)
75 g / 3 oz grated Cheddar cheese
salt and pepper
1 tablespoon olive oil

Cut the baked potatoes in half and scoop out the flesh, leaving enough
round the sides for the skins to keep their shape. Mix the potato with the
flaked tuna, sweetcorn, mayonnaise, milk, spring onion (if using) and 50 g/
2 oz of the grated cheese, and season with a little salt and pepper. Spoon
the filling back into the potato skins, place on a baking tray and drizzle over
the olive oil. Cook for 10 minutes in an oven preheated to 180°C/350°F/
Gas 4 until golden on top.

Stuffed Tomatoes

Another easy dish, which can be prepared in advance and which looks very appealing.

MAKES 2 ADULT PORTIONS

2 eggs
2 medium tomatoes
1 tablespoon mayonnaise

1 tablespoon fresh chives, snipped
salt and pepper

Hard-boil both the eggs. Meanwhile, skin the tomatoes, then cut the tops off and scoop out the inside. Discard the seeds but keep the tiny bits of flesh. When the eggs are ready, peel and mash them together with the pieces of tomato, mayonnaise, chives and a little salt and pepper. Stuff into the tomatoes and replace the tomato tops on the egg mixture.

Delicious Vegetable Rissoles

Nuts and tofu are great for vegetarians as they contain many of the nutrients usually found in animal sources. Tofu and cashew nuts are both excellent source of protein and iron.

MAKES 10 RISSOLES

150 g/5 oz grated carrot
1 medium courgette (approx. 125 g/
4½ oz), topped, tailed and grated
65 g/2½ oz leek, finely chopped
1 garlic clove, crushed
200 g/7 oz chopped button mushrooms
25 g/1 oz butter
200 g/7 oz firm tofu, chopped into pieces

100 g/4 oz unsalted cashew nuts,
finely chopped
100 g/4 oz fresh white breadcrumbs
(made from sliced bread)
1 tablespoon soy sauce
1 tablespoon runny honey
salt and pepper
flour for coating
vegetable oil for frying

Prepare the vegetables and, using your hands, squeeze out any excess liquid from the grated carrot and courgette. Melt the butter in a frying pan and sauté the leek, garlic, carrot and courgette for 2 minutes. Add the mushrooms and cook, stirring occasionally, for 2–3 minutes.

Add the tofu, cashew nuts, breadcrumbs, soy sauce, honey and seasoning, mix well and form into 10 rissoles. Coat in flour and sauté in the oil for about 2 minutes on each side, until golden.

Carrot and Courgette Croquettes

These are quick and easy to make. They are a good way to encourage your child to eat more vegetables and also make a tasty accompaniment to a family meal.

MAKES 6 RISSOLES

75 g / 3 oz carrot, peeled
75 g / 3 oz courgette, trimmed
75 g / 3 oz potato, peeled
1 medium onion, peeled
3 tablespoons ground almonds

2 tablespoons plain flour
2 tablespoons lightly beaten egg
salt and pepper to taste
vegetable oil for frying

Grate the carrot, courgette, potato and onion. Cup small handfuls of the grated vegetables in the palm of your hand and squeeze out the excess moisture. Put the vegetables in a bowl and mix with the almonds, flour and egg. Season to taste. Using your hands, form into six rissoles and sauté in vegetable oil until golden on both sides and cooked through (about 6 minutes).

My Favourite Spanish Omelette

This is good served cold and cut into wedges the next day. I give suggestions on the right for additions to the basic omelette.

MAKES 4 ADULT PORTIONS

3 tablespoons olive oil
175 g/6 oz potatoes, peeled and cut into 1 cm/½ inch cubes
1 onion, peeled and finely chopped
½ small sweet red pepper, deseeded and chopped
50 g/2 oz frozen peas
4 eggs
2 tablespoons Parmesan cheese, grated
salt and pepper

Suggested Variations
2 tablespoons Gruyère instead of Parmesan cheese
1 large chopped tomato
OR
50 g/2 oz mushrooms, sliced
1 tablespoon fresh chives, snipped
OR
100 g/4 oz cooked ham or bacon, cubed
50 g/2 oz sweetcorn instead of peas

Heat the oil in a non-stick 18 cm/ 7 inch frying pan. Fry the potato and onion for 5 minutes, then add the sweet pepper and continue to cook for 5 minutes. Add the peas and cook for a further 5 minutes. Beat the eggs together with 1 tablespoon water and the Parmesan, and season with salt and pepper. Pour this mixture over the vegetables and cook for 5 minutes or until the omelette is almost set. To finish, brown the top under a pre-heated grill for about 3 minutes or until golden. (You can wrap the handle of the frying pan with silver foil to prevent it burning if necessary.) Cut into wedges and serve with salad.

Annabel's Hidden-Vegetable Tomato Sauce

This is the perfect recipe for children who won't eat their vegetables, as all the vegetables are blended into the tomato sauce so they can't be identified or picked out. This tasty sauce can be used as a topping for pizzas or as a sauce for chicken and rice.

MAKES 4 ADULT PORTIONS

2 tablespoons light olive oil
1 garlic clove, crushed
1 medium onion, peeled and finely chopped
100 g/4 oz carrots, peeled and grated
50 g/2 oz courgettes, grated
50 g/2 oz button mushrooms, sliced
1 teaspoon balsamic vinegar

400 g/14 oz passata (ready-sieved tomatoes)
1 teaspoon soft brown sugar
1 vegetable stock cube dissolved in 400 ml/⅔ pint boiling water
a handful fresh basil leaves, torn
salt and freshly ground black pepper

Heat the oil in a saucepan, add the crushed garlic and sauté for a few seconds, then add the onion and sauté for a further 2 minutes. Add the carrots, courgettes and mushrooms and sauté for 4 minutes, stirring occasionally. Add the balsamic vinegar and cook for one minute. Stir in the passata and sugar, cover and simmer for 8 minutes. Add the vegetable stock and cook for 2 minutes, stirring continuously. Add the basil and season to taste. Transfer to a blender and blitz until smooth.

Vegetable Salad with Walnut and Raspberry Dressing

This is a refreshing salad for a summer's lunch. The dressing complements the nutty flavour of the sweetcorn and adds a little sweetness to the salad.

MAKES 4 ADULT PORTIONS

100 g / 4 oz cauliflower, broken into small florets
100 g / 4 oz French beans, trimmed
175 g / 6 oz canned or frozen sweetcorn
sugar and salt to taste
¼ small crisp lettuce, shredded
8 cherry tomatoes, cut in half

1 hard-boiled egg, grated

Dressing
1 tablespoon raspberry vinegar
2 tablespoons walnut or hazelnut oil
salt and pepper to taste

Steam the cauliflower and beans until tender (about 10 minutes). Cook the frozen sweetcorn for about 4 minutes in boiling water with a little sugar and salt. When the cauliflower, beans and sweetcorn have cooled, put all the salad ingredients in a bowl with the grated egg sprinkled on top. Mix the dressing together with a fork and pour it over the salad.

My Favourite Pasta with Broccoli

This is very simple and quick to prepare but it is a great favourite with my three children.

MAKES 4 CHILD PORTIONS

175 g/6 oz fusilli pasta
175 g/6 oz broccoli, cut into florets
25 g/1 oz butter
½ tablespoon sunflower oil

1 onion, peeled and finely chopped
1 garlic clove, peeled and crushed
1 chicken stock cube dissolved in
120 ml/4 fl oz boiling water

Cook the pasta according to the packet instructions. Steam the broccoli for 4 minutes, then set aside. Heat the butter and oil in a wok and sauté the onion and garlic for 3 minutes. Add the steamed broccoli and stir-fry for 1 minute. Stir in the chicken stock, add the cooked, drained pasta and heat through.

Mini Pizzas with Puff Pastry Base

Ready-rolled puff pastry from the supermarket makes a good base for these delicious individual pizzas. You can vary the toppings, maybe adding extras such as mushrooms, ham or pepperoni.

MAKES 4 INDIVIDUAL PIZZAS

1 tablespoon tomato purée
1 tablespoon olive oil
pinch of mixed dried herbs
salt and pepper to taste
350 g/12 oz ready-rolled puff pastry

4 spring onions, trimmed and sliced
4 tablespoons frozen sweetcorn
2 slices salami, cut into thin strips,
or pepperoni (optional)
100 g/4 oz mozzarella cheese, cubed

Place the tomato purée, olive oil and dried herbs in a small saucepan. Season with salt and pepper. Bring to the boil and simmer for 5 minutes until thickened. Cut four 15 cm/6 inch circles out of the pastry (you could cut around a saucer) and place these on an oiled baking sheet. Using a sharp knife, score a circle 5 mm/$\frac{1}{4}$ inch from the edge of the pastry to form a rim.

Divide the tomato mixture between the pastry bases and spread evenly. Sprinkle over the spring onions, sweetcorn and salami (if using) and top with the mozzarella cheese. Season with salt and pepper. Bake in an oven preheated to 180°C/350°F/Gas 4 for 16–18 minutes.

☺ ☹

FISH

Grandma's Gefilte Fish

This is my mother's traditional recipe. It is very appealing to children because of the slightly sweet taste of the balls. My son, Nicholas, loves them and they are very easy for him to hold and eat himself. Adults can eat them with horseradish sauce.

MAKES ABOUT 20 BALLS

*1 onion, peeled and chopped very finely
in the food processor
25 g/1 oz butter
450 g/1 lb minced fish fillet (mix any
of the following: haddock, bream,
whiting, cod or hake)*

*1 egg, beaten
2 dessertspoons sugar
salt and pepper to taste
light cooking oil for frying*

Sauté the onion in the butter until lightly golden. Add to the remaining ingredients and mix well. Shape into golf-ball-sized balls. Fry carefully until golden brown all over. Drain on kitchen paper. Serve hot or cold.

Salmon Fishcakes

Salmon is a good source of omega-3 fatty acids, which are important for brain and visual development. Doctors recommend including at least two oil-rich fish dishes a week to keep the heart in good shape. These fishcakes taste good hot or cold.

MAKES 8 FISHCAKES

300 g/11 oz potatoes, peeled and cut into chunks
15 g/½ oz butter
400 g/14 oz canned red salmon, drained
½ small onion, peeled and finely chopped
2 spring onions, finely chopped

2 tablespoons tomato ketchup
salt and pepper
flour for coating
1 egg, lightly beaten
75 g/3 oz matzo meal or breadcrumbs
oil for frying

Boil the potatoes in a saucepan of lightly salted water. Drain and mash with the butter. Flake the salmon and carefully remove any bones. Mix with the mashed potato, onion, spring onions, tomato ketchup and seasoning. Form into about 8 fishcakes, coat in flour, dip in the egg and then coat in matzo meal or breadcrumbs. Heat the oil in a large frying pan and fry the fishcakes until golden.

Nursery Fish Pie

A good, old-fashioned favourite.

MAKES 6 ADULT PORTIONS

350 g / 12 oz fillet of cod skinned, or
175 g / 6 oz fillets of both cod and salmon
350 ml / 12 fl oz milk
1 bay leaf
4 peppercorns
a sprig of fresh parsley
salt and pepper
25 g / 1 oz butter
25 g / 1 oz plain flour
40 g / 1½ oz grated Cheddar cheese
2 tablespoons fresh chives, snipped

½ tablespoon chopped dill (optional)
2 teaspoons lemon juice
1 hard-boiled egg, chopped
60 g / 2½ oz frozen peas, cooked
following packet instructions

Topping
550 g / 1¼ lb potatoes, peeled and cut
into pieces
40 g / 1½ oz butter
2 tablespoons milk

Put the fish in a saucepan with the milk, bay leaf, peppercorns, parsley and seasoning. Bring to the boil and then simmer, uncovered, for about 5 minutes or until the fish is cooked. While the fish is cooking, cook the potatoes for the topping in boiling, lightly salted water until soft. Drain well, then mash together with 25 g / 1 oz of the butter and the milk.

Drain the fish, reserving the cooking liquid. Melt the butter in a heavy-bottomed saucepan and stir in the flour. Cook gently for 1 minute, then whisk in the fish liquid gradually and bring to the boil. Simmer the sauce for 2–3 minutes until smooth, stirring continuously. Take off the heat and stir in the grated cheese until melted. Break the fish into chunks and fold in together with the chives, dill (if using), lemon juice, boiled egg, peas and seasoning. Place the fish in an ovenproof dish (an 18 cm / 7 inch-diameter and 7½ cm / 3 inch-deep, round dish is perfect) and top with the mashed potato. Bake in the oven preheated to 180°C / 350°F / Gas 4 for 15–20 minutes. Dot with the remaining butter and grill for about 2 minutes until brown and crispy.

Fish in Creamy Mushroom Sauce

For older children, cook 225 g/8 oz fresh spinach and lay each whole fillet on a bed of spinach and pour over the sauce.

MAKES 4 ADULT PORTIONS

1 small onion, peeled and finely chopped
40 g/1½ oz butter
225 g/8 oz button mushrooms, washed
and finely chopped
2 tablespoons lemon juice

2 tablespoons fresh parsley, chopped
2 tablespoons plain flour
300 ml/10 fl oz milk
1 sole or plaice, filleted

Fry the onion in half the butter until transparent. Add the mushrooms, lemon juice and parsley and cook for 2 minutes. Add the flour and cook for 2 minutes, stirring continuously. Add the milk gradually and cook, stirring continuously, until the sauce is thick and smooth.

Fry the sole fillets in the rest of the butter for 2–3 minutes on each side. Cut or flake the fish into small pieces and mix with the mushroom sauce. Alternatively, cover the uncooked fish with the mushroom sauce and bake in the oven preheated to 180°C/350°F/Gas 4 for about 15 minutes or until the fish just flakes.

Gratin of Sole

A very tasty fish recipe which is so easy to make.

MAKES 4 ADULT PORTIONS

4 fillets of lemon sole
salt and pepper to taste
½ small lemon
100 g/4 oz wholemeal breadcrumbs

50 g/2 oz Cheddar cheese, grated
1 heaped tablespoon fresh parsley, chopped
50 g/2 oz margarine, melted

Lay the fillets in a greased ovenproof dish and season with salt, pepper and lemon juice. Put the breadcrumbs, cheese and parsley in a bowl and stir in the melted margarine. Put the breadcrumb mixture on top of the fish in the dish. Place the fish under a preheated grill for about 8 minutes until the breadcrumbs have turned a golden brown and the fish is cooked.

Cod in a Cheese Sauce with Matchstick Vegetables

Cod is particularly delicious roasted in the oven, and here it is served with colourful strips of vegetables and a tasty cheese sauce.

MAKES 2 ADULT PORTIONS

½ small red pepper, cut into thin strips
½ small yellow pepper, cut into thin strips
½ onion, peeled and thinly sliced
1 small courgette, cut into matchsticks
1 tablespoon olive oil
2 x 200 g / 7 oz cod fillets, skinned

salt and pepper
15 g / ½ oz butter
15 g / ½ oz flour
250 ml / 8 fl oz milk
40 g / 1½ oz grated Gruyère cheese
40 g / 1½ oz grated mature Cheddar cheese

Place the vegetable matchsticks in a small roasting tin, drizzle over the olive oil and cook in the oven preheated to 180°C/350°F/Gas 4 for 10 minutes, turning occasionally. Season the cod with salt and pepper and place on top of the vegetables. Return to the oven and cook for a further 10 minutes.

For the sauce, melt the butter in a saucepan and stir in the flour. Cook for 1–2 minutes, then gradually whisk in the milk. Simmer for 2–3 minutes. Stir in the grated cheese until melted. Arrange the vegetables on a plate with a portion of fish on top and pour over some of the cheese sauce.

Chinese-Style Fish Fingers

Although rare, children can be allergic to sesame seeds. Take care, particularly if your child has other food allergies or conditions like eczema or asthma.

MAKES 1 ADULT PORTION

2 fillets of plaice or sole (about 150 g/5 oz), skinned
plain flour
25 g/1 oz butter

1 teaspoon sesame seeds
1 tablespoon finely chopped spring onion
1 tablespoon light soy sauce
2 tablespoons orange juice

Coat the fish in flour and sauté for 2 minutes in the butter with the sesame seeds. Add the remaining ingredients and cook over a low heat for 2–3 minutes or until cooked.

☺ ☹

Salmon and Potato Mash

Salmon is a good source of essential fatty acids, which are important for brain and visual development.

MAKES 2 ADULT PORTIONS

300 g/11 oz potato, peeled and chopped
150 g/5 oz salmon fillet, skinned
40 g/1½ oz butter

2 medium ripe tomatoes, skinned, deseeded and chopped
2 tablespoons milk

Put the potato in the bottom of a steamer, add boiling water, cover and cook for 6 minutes. Place the salmon in the steamer over the potato, cover and cook for another 6 minutes. Meanwhile, melt half the butter and sauté the tomato for 2–3 minutes. Drain the potato and mash together with the remaining butter and milk. Flake the salmon, mix with the tomato and season to taste with salt and pepper. Serve with the mashed potato on the side.

Grandma's Tasty Fish Pie

This is one of my mother's recipes and is a great favourite with all the family. There is never any left the next day.

MAKES 6 ADULT PORTIONS

450 g / 1 lb cod or haddock fillets, skinned
seasoned flour
1 egg, lightly beaten
100 g / 4 oz fine breadcrumbs
vegetable oil
1 onion, peeled and finely chopped
1½ tablespoons olive oil
75 g / 3 oz green sweet pepper, cored,
deseeded and chopped
150 g / 5 oz sweet red pepper, cored,
deseeded and chopped

400 g / 14 oz canned tomatoes
2 tablespoons tomato purée
½ teaspoon soft brown sugar
salt and pepper

Cheese Sauce
25 g / 1 oz butter
1 tablespoon plain flour
250 ml / 8 fl oz milk
75 g / 3 oz Cheddar cheese, grated
40 g / 1½ oz Parmesan cheese, grated

Preheat the oven to 180°C/350°F/Gas 4. Cut the fish fillets into about 12 pieces, dip in seasoned flour, then into the lightly beaten egg, and finally coat in breadcrumbs. Sauté in the vegetable oil until golden on both sides. Drain on kitchen paper.

Sauté the onion in the olive oil for 3–4 minutes. Add the peppers and cook for 5 minutes. Drain half of the juice from the tomatoes, then add the tomatoes and the remaining juice to the peppers with the tomato purée and sugar. Season to taste and cook for about 5 minutes. Mix the cooked fish with the tomato sauce and transfer to an ovenproof dish.

Make a cheese sauce with the butter, flour and milk, stirring over a low heat until smooth and thick (see page 59). Remove from the heat and stir in two-thirds of the Cheddar and Parmesan.

Pour the cheese sauce over the fish fillets. Sprinkle with the remaining grated cheese and bake in the preheated oven for about 20 minutes. Brown under a hot grill.

Kids' Kedgeree

This is a really scrummy kedgeree, which makes a great family meal that is popular with kids. It's the kind of food you could eat for breakfast or supper. If you want to make a smaller amount, simply halve the quantities.

MAKES 6 ADULT PORTIONS

350 g / 12 oz undyed smoked haddock
100 ml / 3½ fl oz double cream
25 g / 1 oz butter
1 onion, peeled and chopped
1 teaspoon mild curry paste

200 g / 7 oz basmati rice, cooked
1 teaspoon lemon juice
2 tablespoons fresh parsley, chopped
2 hard-boiled eggs, chopped
salt and pepper

Place the haddock in a microwave-proof dish and pour over the cream. Cover with clingfilm, pierce a few times with the tip of a sharp knife and place in the microwave on High for 5–6 minutes. Meanwhile, in a frying pan or wok, melt the butter and sauté the onion for 8 minutes until soft. Stir in the curry paste and rice and cook for 1 minute, stirring continuously. Flake in the haddock and add the cooking liquor, lemon juice, parsley and chopped eggs. Season with salt and pepper if necessary.

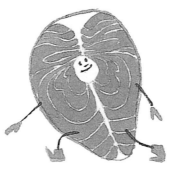

Toasted Tuna Muffins

A can of tuna in the larder is a good standby and tuna is rich in protein, Vitamin D and Vitamin B12. These toasted muffins are quick and easy to make for a tasty and healthy meal.

MAKES 1–2 PORTIONS

100 g/4 oz canned tuna in oil, drained
1 tablespoon mayonnaise
1 tablespoon tomato ketchup
1 spring onion, finely chopped

2 tablespoons canned sweetcorn
1 English muffin
25 g/1 oz grated Cheddar cheese

Flake the tuna into a bowl and stir in the mayonnaise, tomato ketchup, spring onion and sweetcorn. Preheat the grill, divide the muffin into 2 halves and toast. Divide the tuna mixture between the 2 halves. Cover with the grated cheese and place under the grill for about 2 minutes until golden and bubbling.

Tuna Pitta Pocket

MAKES 2 PITTA POCKETS

100 g/4 oz canned tuna in oil, drained
50 g/2 oz sweetcorn
1 hard-boiled egg, chopped
1 tablespoon mayonnaise
½ teaspoon white wine vinegar

2 spring onions, chopped
1 tomato, skinned, deseeded and chopped
salt and freshly ground black pepper
1 pitta bread

Flake the tuna with a fork and mix with the sweetcorn, hard-boiled egg, mayonnaise, white wine vinegar, spring onions, tomato and seasoning. Toast the pitta bread, cut in half to make two pockets and divide the mixture between them.

Tuna Tagliatelle

This is my favourite tuna recipe.

MAKES 6 ADULT PORTIONS

½ onion, peeled and finely chopped
25 g / 1 oz butter
1 tablespoon cornflour
120 ml / 4 fl oz water
400 g / 14 oz canned cream of tomato
soup
a pinch of mixed dried herbs
1 tablespoon fresh parsley, chopped
200 g / 7 oz canned tuna, drained and
flaked
black pepper

175 g / 6 oz green tagliatelle
1 tablespoon grated Parmesan cheese

Mushroom Cheese Sauce
½ onion, peeled and finely chopped
40 g / 1½ oz butter
100 g / 4 oz mushrooms, washed and
sliced
2 tablespoons plain flour
300 ml / 10 fl oz milk
100 g / 4 oz Cheddar cheese, grated

For the sauce, fry the onion in the butter until transparent, then add the sliced mushrooms and sauté for about 3 minutes. Add the flour and continue stirring the mixture all the time. When it is well mixed, add the milk gradually and cook, stirring until thickened and smooth. Remove from the heat and stir in the grated cheese.

Fry the onion in the butter until soft. Stir the cornflour into the water until dissolved, and mix with the tomato soup. Add the mixed dried herbs and fresh parsley and cook, stirring, over a low heat for 5 minutes. Mix in the flaked tuna and heat through. Season with a little black pepper.

Boil the tagliatelle in water until *al dente*, then drain. Grease a serving dish and add the tuna and tomato mixed with the pasta and then the mushroom cheese sauce. Top with grated Parmesan. Bake in an oven pre-heated to 180°C/350°F/Gas 4 for 20 minutes. Brown under a hot grill before serving.

Tuna with Pasta and Tomatoes

Most children like penne with tomato sauce, and it's a good idea to add
some canned tuna and grated cheese to boost the nutritional content.
Semi-dried sunblush tomatoes add a lovely flavour to this dish.

MAKES 6 ADULT PORTIONS

200 g / 7 oz penne
2 tablespoons olive oil
1 medium red onion, peeled and chopped
1 garlic clove, crushed
*½ medium red pepper, cored, deseeded
and chopped*
100 g / 4 oz button mushrooms
800 g / 28 oz canned chopped tomatoes

100 g / 4 oz sunblush tomatoes, chopped
*400 g / 14 oz canned tuna in sunflower
oil, drained*
2 teaspoons balsamic vinegar
½ teaspoon mixed dried herbs
a handful fresh basil leaves, torn
150 g / 5 oz Cheddar cheese, grated

Cook the penne according to the packet instructions. In a large saucepan,
heat the oil and sauté the onion, garlic and red pepper for 5 minutes,
stirring occasionally. Add the mushrooms and cook for a further 3 minutes.
Add the canned tomatoes, sunblush tomatoes, flaked tuna, balsamic vinegar
and dried herbs and cook for 10 minutes uncovered. Stir in the drained,
cooked pasta and the fresh basil.

Transfer to a fairly shallow ovenproof dish and sprinkle with the grated
cheese. Preheat the grill on a high setting and cook for about 3 minutes or
until golden and bubbling.

CHICKEN

Thai-Style Chicken and Noodles

Don't be afraid to try out new tastes on your child – this recipe flavoured with mild curry and coconut sauce is very popular. Young children often surprise us and like quite sophisticated foods and it's usually easier to get children to accept new tastes whilst they are young. This would make a good meal for the whole family.

MAKES 4 PORTIONS

Marinade
1 tablespoon soy sauce
1 tablespoon sake
½ teaspoon sugar
1 teaspoon cornflour

1½ chicken breasts cut into strips
125 g/4½ oz Chinese noodles
1 tablespoon vegetable oil
3 spring onions, sliced

1 garlic clove, crushed
½ teaspoon red chilli, deseeded and chopped
1½–2 teaspoons korma curry paste
150 ml/5 fl oz chicken stock (see page 62)
150 ml/5 fl oz coconut milk
75 g/3 oz baby corn cobs, cut into quarters
100 g/4 oz beansprouts
75 g/3 oz frozen peas

Mix together the ingredients for the marinade and marinate the chicken for at least 30 minutes. Cook the noodles according to the packet instructions, drain and rinse under cold water. Heat the vegetable oil in a wok or frying pan and stir-fry the spring onions, garlic and chilli for about 2 minutes. Drain the marinade from the chicken, add to the wok and continue to stir-fry for 2 minutes. Add the curry paste, chicken stock and coconut milk and cook for 5 minutes over a low heat. Add the baby corn and beansprouts and cook for 3–4 minutes. Finally, add the peas and cook for 2 minutes more.

Bar-B-Q Chicken

A good marinade will transform your barbecue, tenderising the meat, as well as adding a delicious flavour. I use a Weber Bar-B-Q, which has a cover, enabling me to barbecue all year round, even in England. Use 900 g/2 lb breast of chicken, skinned and on the bone, with these marinades – they also work well with beef or lamb.

MAKES 4–5 ADULT PORTIONS

Hoisin Marinade
2 tablespoons soy sauce
2 tablespoons hoisin sauce
2 tablespoons rice wine vinegar
1 tablespoon honey
1 tablespoon vegetable oil
½ teaspoon crushed garlic (optional)

Teriyaki Marinade
3 tablespoons rice wine vinegar or white wine vinegar
2 tablespoons soy sauce
1 tablespoon honey
½ tablespoon sesame oil
1 teaspoon grated ginger root (optional)
1 tablespoon sliced spring onion

Mix all the marinade ingredients together. Marinate the chicken for at least 2 hours, then barbecue, basting and turning occasionally for 15–25 minutes. Dark meat takes longer to cook than white meat. Chicken should be cooked through, but not overcooked or it will become dry. If you are unsure about cooking meat thoroughly before the surface is charred, cook it in an oven preheated to 200°C/400°F/Gas 6 for 25–30 minutes and finish it on the barbecue for a few minutes to give an authentic flavour.

Chicken Satay

These barbecued chicken skewers are fun to eat and very popular with toddlers. Help your child take the meat off the skewers, then remove the skewers – they could become dangerous in the hands of exuberant toddlers.

MAKES 2 ADULT PORTIONS

2 chicken breasts, off the bone
1 small onion, peeled
1 small sweet red pepper, deseeded

Marinade
2 tablespoons peanut butter
1 tablespoon chicken stock (see page 62)
1 tablespoon rice wine vinegar
1 tablespoon honey
1 tablespoon soy sauce
1 teaspoon crushed garlic (optional)
1 teaspoon sesame seeds, toasted
(optional, see page 138)

Mix together the marinade ingredients. Soak 4 bamboo skewers in water to prevent them getting scorched. Cut the chicken, onion and pepper into chunks. Leave the chicken in the marinade for at least 2 hours. Thread with the onion and pepper onto the skewers (or just use chicken). Cook under a preheated grill for about 5 minutes each side, basting occasionally. Alternatively, cook on a barbecue.

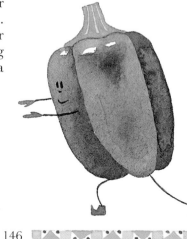

Peanuts can cause allergic reactions (see page 15).

Chicken Soup with Pasta and Vegetables

This is a very quick and easy chicken noodle soup that is very popular with my three children. Vermicelli is very fine pasta that comes rolled up in nests.

MAKES 6 PORTIONS

1 litre / 1³/4 pints chicken stock
1 tablespoon vegetable oil
1 onion, peeled and thinly sliced
1 garlic clove, crushed
125 g / 4¹/₂ oz chicken breast, cut into bite-sized pieces

¹/₄ teaspoon chicken seasoning
50 g / 2 oz green beans, topped, tailed and cut into short lengths
50 g / 2 oz vermicelli or tiny pasta stars
1 tomato, skinned, deseeded and chopped

Make up the chicken stock in a pan using either 2 chicken stock cubes and boiling water, liquid stock from a supermarket or my recipe on page 62. Meanwhile, heat the vegetable oil in another saucepan and sauté the onion and garlic for 2 minutes. Add the chicken, sprinkle with chicken seasoning and sauté for 1 minute, stirring occasionally, then add the green beans and sauté for 3 minutes. Mix the chicken, onion, green beans and vermicelli with the chicken stock. Bring to the boil, then reduce the heat and cook for 3–4 minutes or until the pasta is cooked and the beans are just tender. Stir in the chopped tomato and cook for 1 minute.

Chicken Fillets with Mango Chutney and Apricot

This is very simple to prepare, but tastes absolutely delicious. It is a great favourite with children because of the sweet-and-sour taste.

MAKES 2 ADULT PORTIONS

2 chicken breasts, off the bone and skinned

Sauce
1 tablespoon apricot jam
1 tablespoon mango chutney
3 tablespoons mayonnaise
1 teaspoon Worcestershire sauce
1 tablespoon lemon juice

Mix all the ingredients together for the sauce. Put the chicken into a small ovenproof dish, pour over the sauce and cover the dish with aluminium foil. Bake in an oven preheated to 180°C/350°F/Gas 4 for 30 minutes.

Stir-Fried Chicken with Vegetables and Noodles

Stir-fries are popular with children and make great family food. To save time you could try using a pack of ready prepared stir-fry vegetables from the supermarket and then just add a few extra favourite vegetables of your own.

MAKES 4 ADULT PORTIONS

Marinade
1½ tablespoons soy sauce
1 tablespoon sake
1 teaspoon sesame oil
1 tablespoon white wine vinegar
1 teaspoon soft brown sugar
1 teaspoon cornflour

2 skinned chicken breasts, cut into strips
100 g/4 oz fine Chinese noodles
3 tablespoons vegetable oil

1 onion, peeled and finely sliced
1 garlic clove, peeled and crushed
75 g/3 oz carrot, cut into matchsticks
75 g/3 oz baby corn, cut into quarters
75 g/3 oz broccoli, cut into florets
100 g/4 oz courgette, trimmed and cut into matchsticks
100 g/4 oz beansprouts
1 chicken stock cube dissolved in 175 ml/6 fl oz boiling water
salt and freshly ground black pepper

Mix the marinade ingredients and marinate the chicken for at least 30 minutes. Cook the noodles according to the packet instructions, then drain and stir in a little oil to prevent them sticking. Strain the marinade from the chicken and reserve. Heat 1 tablespoon of the oil in a wok and stir-fry the chicken for 4–6 minutes until cooked through, then set aside. Heat the remaining oil in the wok and sauté the onion and garlic for 3 minutes. Add the carrot, baby corn and broccoli and stir-fry for 3 minutes. Add the courgette and beansprouts and stir-fry for 2 minutes. Pour the chicken stock into a small saucepan and add the reserved marinade. Bring to the boil, stirring until thickened. Season with a little salt and pepper. Add the chicken and noodles to the stir-fried vegetables, pour over the sauce and heat through.

Mulligatawny Chicken

This recipe has a tomato base and a mild curry flavour that children love. It has been a family favourite since I was a child and was invented by my mother. It is best served with rice and, for special occasions, you can serve *poppadoms* as an accompaniment. They are available in most supermarkets.

MAKES 8 ADULT PORTIONS

1 chicken, cut into about 10 pieces, skinned
seasoned flour
vegetable oil
2 medium onions, peeled and chopped
6 tablespoons tomato purée
2 tablespoons mild curry powder
900 ml/1½ pints chicken stock (see page 62)

1 large or 2 small apples, cored and thinly sliced
1 small carrot, peeled and thinly sliced
2 lemon slices
75 g/3 oz sultanas
1 bay leaf
1 dessertspoon brown sugar
salt and pepper

Coat the chicken pieces with seasoned flour. Fry in vegetable oil until golden brown. Drain on kitchen paper and place in a casserole dish.

Fry the onion in a little oil until golden, then stir in the tomato purée. Add the curry powder and continue to stir for a couple of minutes over a low heat. Stir in 2 tablespoons of flour, then pour in 300 ml/10 fl oz of the stock, mixing well.

Add the apple, carrot, lemon slices, sultanas, bay leaf and the rest of the stock. Season with brown sugar, salt and pepper. Pour the sauce over the chicken in the casserole, cover and cook for 1 hour in an oven pre-heated to 180°C/350°F/Gas 4. Remove the lemon slices and bay leaf; take the chicken off the bone and cut it into pieces.

☺ ☹ ❄

Sesame Chicken Nuggets with Chinese Sauce

These crisp sesame-coated nuggets in a tasty sauce are very popular. They are good served with Special Fried Rice (see page 123). It's fun for children to eat these with chopsticks – you can buy plastic chopsticks that are joined together at the top and are very easy for children to use. Sesame seeds can cause an allergic reaction in young children. Although this is very rare, watch your child closely, particularly if he is allergic to any other foods, or has any conditions such as eczema or asthma.

MAKES 12 NUGGETS

2 chicken breasts, off the bone and
skinned
1 egg
1 tablespoon milk
seasoned flour
100 g/4 oz sesame seeds
2 tablespoons vegetable oil

Chinese Sauce
250 ml/8 fl oz unsalted chicken stock
(see page 62)
2 teaspoons soy sauce
1 teaspoon sesame oil
1 tablespoon caster sugar
1 teaspoon cider vinegar
1 tablespoon cornflour
1 spring onion, finely sliced

Cut each chicken breast into about six pieces. Beat the egg together with the milk and dip the nuggets into seasoned flour, then into the egg and finally coat with sesame seeds. Fry in hot oil for about 5 minutes, turning the chicken frequently, until golden brown and cooked through. Mix together all the ingredients for the sauce, apart from the spring onion, in a small saucepan. Bring to the boil and then simmer for 2–3 minutes or until thickened. Add the spring onion and pour the sauce over the chicken and heat through.

☺	☹	❄

Marinated Chicken on the Griddle

I love cooking chicken, meat or fish on a griddle, and it's a very healthy way of cooking as it uses very little fat. My three children love this recipe as marinating the chicken gives it a lovely flavour and makes it more tender. Make sure the griddle is really hot before you lay the food on it.

MAKES 2 ADULT PORTIONS

2 chicken breasts
1 tablespoon olive oil

1 tablespoon soy sauce
1 tablespoon honey
1 small garlic clove, peeled and sliced
2 sprigs of fresh rosemary (optional)

Marinade
juice of ½ lemon

Score the chicken breasts 2 or 3 times with a sharp knife. Mix together all the ingredients for the marinade and marinate the chicken for at least 2 hours. Heat the griddle, brush with oil, then remove the chicken from the marinade and cook for 4 –5 minutes on each side or until cooked through. Cut into strips and serve with vegetables and chips or mashed potato. Serve with colourful vegetables such as carrots, broccoli or peas.

RED MEAT
Annabel's Tasty Beefburgers

The grated apple makes these beefburgers really moist and tasty. Serve in a bun with salad and ketchup, and some oven-baked chips They are also good cooked on a barbecue in summer.

MAKES 8 BURGERS

½ red pepper, cored, deseeded and chopped
1 onion, peeled and finely chopped
1 tablespoon vegetable oil
450 g / 1 lb lean minced beef or lamb
1 tablespoon fresh parsley, chopped
1 chicken stock cube, finely crumbled
1 apple, peeled and grated

1 egg, lightly beaten
25 g / 1 oz fresh breadcrumbs
1 teaspoon Worcestershire sauce
salt and freshly ground black pepper
a little plain flour
vegetable oil for brushing a griddle pan or for frying

Fry the red pepper and half the onion in the vegetable oil for about 5 minutes or until softened. In a mixing bowl, combine the sautéed onion, pepper and remaining raw onion with all the ingredients except for the flour and vegetable oil. With floured hands, form into 8 burgers. Brush a griddle pan with a little oil and, when hot, place 4 burgers on the griddle and cook for about 5 minutes each side or until browned and cooked through. Repeat with the remaining burgers. Alternatively, fry in a little hot oil in a shallow frying pan. Serve the burgers on their own or in a toasted hamburger bun with salad and ketchup.

☺	☹	❄

Cocktail Meatballs with Tomato Sauce

These meatballs can be served on their own without the sauce and make tasty finger food. They are also good served with spaghetti or rice.

MAKES 6 PORTIONS

Tomato Sauce
1½ tablespoons light olive oil
1 medium onion, peeled and chopped
1 garlic clove, crushed
250 g/9 oz fresh ripe tomatoes, skinned, deseeded and chopped
400 g/14 oz canned tomatoes, chopped
1 teaspoon balsamic vinegar
1 teaspoon caster sugar
salt and freshly ground black pepper
1 tablespoon fresh basil, torn

Meatballs
450 g/1 lb lean minced beef
1 medium onion, peeled and finely chopped
1 Granny Smith apple, peeled and grated
50 g/2 oz fresh white breadcrumbs
1 tablespoon fresh parsley, chopped
1 chicken stock cube, finely crumbled and dissolved in 2 tablespoons boiling water
salt and freshly ground black pepper
plain flour for forming meatballs
vegetable oil for frying

To make the tomato sauce, heat the oil in a saucepan and gently cook the onion and garlic until softened. Stir in the fresh tomatoes and cook for 1 minute. Add the canned tomatoes, vinegar, sugar and seasoning and cook for 20 minutes over a low heat. Add the basil and then blend in a food processor to make a smooth sauce.

Meanwhile, mix together the ingredients for the meatballs. Using floured hands, form into about 24 balls. Heat the oil in a frying pan and sauté the meatballs over a fairly high heat, turning occasionally, until browned, then reduce the heat and continue to cook for about 5 minutes. Pour over the tomato sauce and continue to cook, covered, for 10–15 minutes.

Shepherd's Pie

If you have any little ramekin dishes, then it is very nice to make your child his very own little shepherd's pie. Let him see it, and then spoon out of the hot dish onto his plate.

MAKES 4 ADULT PORTIONS

1 onion, peeled and finely chopped
1 sweet red pepper, deseeded and finely chopped
1 tablespoon fresh parsley, finely chopped
2 tablespoons vegetable oil
450 g / 1 lb lean minced beef
250 ml / 8 fl oz chicken stock (see page 62)
1 teaspoon Marmite
salt and pepper

100 g / 4 oz button mushrooms, washed and sliced
15 g / ½ oz margarine or butter

Topping
450 g / 1 lb potatoes, peeled and chopped
25 g / 1 oz butter
50 ml / 2 fl oz milk
salt and pepper

Fry the chopped onion, pepper and parsley in the oil until softened. Meanwhile, in a frying pan, brown the mince. Put the meat into a food processor for 30 seconds to make it easier to chew. Add to the pan with the onion mixture and stir in the chicken stock, Marmite and seasoning. Cook over a low heat for about 20 minutes. Meanwhile, sauté the mushrooms in the margarine or butter and add these to the meat when it is cooked.

To make the topping, boil the potatoes in lightly salted water for about 15 minutes or until tender. Mash them together with half the butter, milk and some salt and pepper. Spread over the meat either in one large dish or individual ramekins, then cook in an oven preheated to 180°C/350°F/ Gas 4 for 10 minutes. Dot the top with the remaining butter and put under a hot grill for about 3 minutes or until golden.

☺ ☹

Mini Minute Steaks

These mini steaks with a delicious gravy and sautéed potatoes are
absolutely delicious.

MAKES 2 ADULT OR 4 CHILD PORTIONS

2 tablespoons vegetable oil
1 onion, peeled and thinly sliced
1 teaspoon caster sugar
1 tablespoon water
200 ml/7 fl oz beef stock
1 teaspoon cornflour mixed with
1 tablespoon water

a few drops of Worcestershire sauce
1 teaspoon tomato purée
salt and pepper
350 g/12 oz peeled potatoes
25 g/1 oz butter
4 x 60 g/2½ oz minute steaks (fillet or
rump), about 5 mm/¼ inch thick

To make the gravy, heat 1 tablespoon of the vegetable oil in a frying
pan. Add the onion and cook for 7–8 minutes until just turning
golden brown. Stir in the sugar and water, increase the heat and cook
for about 1 minute until the water has evaporated. Stir in the beef stock,
cornflour mixed with 1 tablespoon water, Worcestershire sauce and tomato
purée. Season with salt and pepper. Cook, stirring, for 2–3 minutes until
thickened.

For the sautéed potatoes, cut the potatoes into large chunks, bring to the
boil in lightly salted water and cook for about 8 minutes until they are just
tender. Drain and cut into 1 cm/½ inch thick slices. Heat the butter in a
frying pan and sauté the potatoes for 5–6 minutes, turning occasionally
until golden brown and crispy.

Heat the remaining oil in a frying pan, season the steaks and fry for
1–2 minutes each side. Serve with the gravy and sautéed potatoes.

☺ ☹

Veal Stroganoff

Veal is easier than beef for your toddler to chew. This recipe is quick and easy to make – and delicious. It is very nice as a family meal served with noodles and, to give it an authentic stroganoff taste, you can even add a dollop of soured cream.

MAKES 2 ADULT PORTIONS

cooking oil
1 onion, peeled and very finely chopped
½ red and ½ yellow sweet pepper,
deseeded and cut into strips
225 g/8 oz thin veal escalope, cut
into strips

seasoned flour
300 ml/10 fl oz chicken stock (see
page 62)
175 g/6 oz button mushrooms, washed
and sliced
salt and pepper

Heat a little oil in a frying pan and sauté the onion for 3–4 minutes. Add the strips of sweet pepper and continue to cook for 1 more minute. Roll the strips of veal in seasoned flour and cook these in the frying pan for about 3 minutes or until browned (add a little more oil if you find the veal is sticking to the pan).

Pour the chicken stock over the veal and stir in the mushrooms and some salt and pepper. Simmer, covered, for about 8 minutes.

157

Sticky Chops

MAKES 2 ADULT PORTIONS

Marinade
2 tablespoons tomato ketchup
1 tablespoon soy sauce
1 tablespoon runny honey
1 teaspoon lemon juice

a few drops of Worcestershire sauce
a little freshly ground black pepper

4 lamb chops or lamb cutlets

Mix together all of the ingredients for the marinade, add the lamb chops and leave to marinate for 1–2 hours at room temperature or overnight in the fridge. Place on a grill pan under a medium-high grill for 4–5 minutes each side, basting with any remaining marinade.

Liver and Onion

You are doing a great job if your children enjoy liver.

MAKES 1–2 ADULT PORTIONS

½ onion, peeled and chopped
1 tablespoon finely chopped green sweet pepper
vegetable oil

2 tablespoons chopped mushrooms
1 medium tomato, skinned, deseeded and chopped
100 g/4 oz calf's liver

Fry the chopped onion and pepper in a little oil until the onions are very brown. Add the chopped mushrooms and tomato and fry for another 2 minutes. Fry the liver for 1½ minutes each side. When the liver is cooked, cut into small pieces and cover with the vegetables.

PASTA
Spaghetti with Two-Tomato Sauce

A really good home-made tomato sauce is always popular – and it can be served with any type of pasta and maybe freshly grated Parmesan cheese.

MAKES 4 CHILD PORTIONS

3 tablespoons olive oil
1 onion, peeled and chopped
1 garlic clove, peeled and crushed
4 ripe tomatoes, skinned, deseeded and chopped
400 g/14 oz canned chopped tomatoes

pinch of sugar
1 bay leaf
2 tablespoons fresh basil, chopped
salt and pepper
250 g/9 oz spaghetti

Heat the oil in a saucepan and sauté the onion and garlic for 5–6 minutes until softened. Add the fresh and canned tomatoes, sugar, bay leaf and chopped basil, then season with salt and pepper. Bring to a simmer and cook for 20 minutes. Meanwhile, cook the spaghetti according to the packet instructions. Drain the pasta and mix with the sauce.

Bow-Ties with Gruyère and Cherry Tomatoes

This is a great favourite with my children and can be eaten either warm or cold.

MAKES 4 CHILD PORTIONS

175 g/6 oz bow-tie pasta
1 tablespoon white wine vinegar
3 tablespoons olive oil
½ teaspoon Dijon mustard (optional)
a pinch of sugar

a little salt and freshly ground black pepper
1 tablespoon fresh chives, snipped
100 g/4 oz cherry tomatoes, halved or quartered
50 g/2 oz Gruyère cheese, grated

Cook the pasta in lightly salted water according to the packet instructions. Make a vinaigrette by mixing together the vinegar, oil, mustard (if using), sugar and seasoning, then add the snipped chives. Drain the pasta and put into a bowl, then mix with the cherry tomatoes and grated Gruyère cheese. Shake the vinaigrette, pour over the pasta and toss well to coat.

Fluffy Macaroni Cheese

Whipped egg whites give this tasty macaroni cheese a lovely light texture.

MAKES 4 PORTIONS

175 g/6 oz macaroni
25 g/1 oz butter
25 g/1 oz flour
275 ml/10 fl oz milk
a little nutmeg, grated
60 g/2 oz mascarpone cheese

50 g/2 oz Cheddar cheese, grated
25 g/1 oz Gruyère cheese, grated
2 eggs, separated
salt and freshly ground black pepper
4 tablespoons Parmesan cheese, freshly grated

Cook the macaroni according to the packet instructions. Use the butter, flour, milk and nutmeg to make a thick white sauce (see page 59). Remove from the heat and whisk in the Cheddar and Gruyère until melted, and then the mascarpone and egg yolks. Season with salt and pepper.

Whisk the egg whites to form soft peaks and gently fold into the sauce. Drain the pasta, mix with the sauce and spoon into an ovenproof dish. Sprinkle the Parmesan on top and place in an oven preheated to 180°C/350°F/Gas 4 for 12–15 minutes until lightly golden.

Spaghetti Primavera

A simple recipe for spaghetti with spring vegetables in a tasty cheese sauce. You could also make this with pasta shapes.

MAKES 4 PORTIONS

150 g/5 oz spaghetti
1 tablespoon olive oil
1 onion, chopped
1 garlic clove, crushed
1 medium carrot (approx. 75 g/3 oz) cut into matchsticks
1 medium courgette (approx. 75 g/3 oz) cut into matchsticks

125 g/4½ oz cauliflower cut into small florets
150 ml/5 fl oz light crème fraîche
150 ml/5 fl oz vegetable stock (see page 33)
50 g/2 oz frozen peas
50 g/2 oz fresh Parmesan cheese, grated

Cook the spaghetti according to the packet instructions. Heat the oil in a heavy-bottomed saucepan and sauté the onion and garlic for 1 minute. Add the carrot and courgette matchsticks and sauté, stirring occasionally, for 2–3 minutes. Meanwhile, blanch the cauliflower in lightly salted boiling water for 5 minutes or steam until tender. Add the crème fraîche, vegetable stock and peas to the carrot and courgette and stir in. Cook for 2–3 minutes before stirring in the Parmesan. Drain the spaghetti and toss with the sauce.

Bow-Ties with Tomato and Mozzarella Sauce

A very tasty easy to prepare tomato sauce enriched with two cheeses.

MAKES 4 CHILD PORTIONS

150 g/5 oz bow-tie pasta
2 tablespoons olive oil
1 onion, peeled and chopped
1 garlic clove, peeled and crushed
400 g/14 oz canned chopped tomatoes
1 teaspoon balsamic vinegar
a pinch of sugar

1 tablespoon fresh basil, torn
100 ml/3½ fl oz vegetable stock (see page 33)
100 g/4 oz mozzarella cheese, diced
3 tablespoons Parmesan cheese, grated
salt and pepper

Cook the pasta according to the packet directions. To make the sauce, heat the olive oil in a saucepan and sauté the onion and garlic for 5–6 minutes until softened. Stir in the chopped tomatoes, balsamic vinegar, sugar, basil and stock and simmer for 10 minutes. Stir in the mozzarella and Parmesan cheese. Season to taste and mix with the bow-tie pasta.

Animal Pasta Salad with Multicoloured Vegetables

I make this recipe with multicoloured animal-shaped pasta. Toddlers love picking out all the different ingredients. It looks very attractive and colourful on a plate and can be served warm or cold. You can omit the chicken for a vegetarian dish.

MAKES 4 CHILD PORTIONS

100 g/4 oz multicoloured pasta shapes
1 chicken breast, skinned and cut into bite-sized pieces
vegetable oil
3 baby carrots or 1 medium carrot, cut into fine strips
50 g/2 oz each broccoli and cauliflower, broken into small florets
3 courgettes, trimmed and sliced
50 g/2 oz French beans, chopped
100 g/4 oz frozen sweetcorn

½ sweet red pepper, finely chopped
salt
sugar

Dressing
2 tablespoons cider vinegar or red wine vinegar
salt and black pepper
50 ml/2 fl oz olive oil
2 spring onions, finely sliced, or 2 tablespoons fresh chives, snipped

Cook the pasta according to the packet instructions and drain. Fry the chicken in a little oil for 2 minutes, then add the carrots and continue to cook for a further 5 minutes. Meanwhile steam the broccoli, cauliflower, courgettes and beans until cooked but still crisp. The broccoli and cauliflower will need a little longer than the courgettes and beans. Cook the sweetcorn and red pepper in water with a little salt and sugar for 5 minutes.

To prepare the dressing, whisk the vinegar with salt and pepper, then whisk in the olive oil a little at a time. Add the spring onions. Combine all the ingredients together and pour the dressing over.

FRUIT AND DESSERTS

Poached Fruits

MAKES 4 ADULT PORTIONS

*2 large or 3 small pears, peeled,
quartered and cored
150 g/5 oz plums, halved and stoned
150 g/5 oz blackberries*

*75 ml/3 fl oz apple juice
60 g/2½ oz caster sugar
1 small stick cinnamon
100 g/4 oz raspberries*

Cut the pear quarters in half and place in a large saucepan. Add the plums, blackberries, apple juice, caster sugar and the cinnamon stick. Bring to a gentle simmer and cover with a lid for 10 minutes. Stir in the raspberries. Remove the cinnamon stick before serving and serve chilled.

Peach Melba Delight

A healthy alternative to this favourite ice-cream dessert.

MAKES 1 ADULT PORTION

*100 g/4 oz raspberries, fresh or frozen
2 teaspoons caster sugar
1 small carton mild natural yoghurt*

*1 ripe peach, skinned, stoned and cut
into small pieces*

Put the raspberries and sugar in a small saucepan and cook gently for 2–3 minutes or until soft and mushy. Press the raspberries through a sieve and mix together with the yoghurt and chopped peach.

Snow-Covered Fruit Salad

Try this combination of fruits, which are all rich in Vitamin C – better than any vitamin tablets. You can make your own combination according to what is in season. Scoop the melon into small balls if you have a melon scooper.

MAKES 5 ADULT PORTIONS

1 peach, skinned, stoned and cut into small pieces
1 papaya, peeled, deseeded and cut into small chunks
8 strawberries, hulled and cut into quarters
2 oranges, peeled, pith removed and cut into chunks
1 tablespoon raspberries or blackberries
½ small cantaloupe melon, flesh removed and cut into chunks
100 g / 4 oz cherries, stoned and halved,

or 100 g / 4 oz blueberries
1 small wedge of watermelon, flesh removed and cut into chunks
2 kiwi fruit, peeled and sliced
juice of 1 orange

Topping
450 ml / 16 fl oz natural yoghurt
2 tablespoons honey
2 tablespoons wheat germ or muesli (optional)

Combine all the fruits together in a large bowl. Pour the orange juice over them and mix well.

Mix the yoghurt with the honey and wheat germ or muesli (if using), and pour over the fruit just before serving.

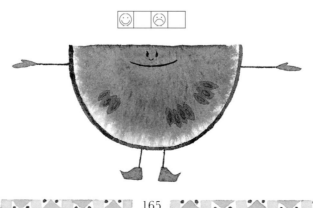

Peaches with Amaretti Biscuits

Amaretti biscuits are small round macaroons from Italy, and can be bought in most supermarkets. This delicious fruit dessert can be made with many different fruits. Try a combination of white peaches and raspberries or sliced plums. You could also make this dessert using light crème fraîche.

MAKES 2 ADULT PORTIONS

2 large ripe peaches, stoned and sliced
25 g / 1 oz crushed amaretti biscuits

125 ml / 4½ fl oz crème fraîche
1 heaped tablespoon brown sugar

Place the sliced peaches in a shallow ovenproof dish and sprinkle with the crushed amaretti biscuits. Cover with the crème fraîche and then sprinkle over the brown sugar. Place under a preheated grill for about 6 minutes until golden.

☺ ☹

Pear, Apple and Raspberry Crumble

A really good crumble bursting with fruit is comfort food at its very best; and it is easy to prepare and always a great favourite with the family. I like to choose fruits that have a slightly tart flavour. Rhubarb with 50 g/2 oz brown sugar and a few tablespoons of orange juice makes a good fruit crumble, and the apple and blackberry mixture on page 86 mixed with 100 g/4 oz light muscovado sugar is also delicious. Crumbles are best served hot with custard or vanilla ice cream.

MAKES 6 ADULT PORTIONS

2 eating apples, peeled and chopped
2 ripe pears, peeled and chopped
250 g/9 oz raspberries, fresh or frozen
1 tablespoon caster sugar

Crumble Topping
150 g/5 oz plain flour
a pinch of salt
100 g/4 oz cold butter, cut into pieces
75 g/3 oz soft brown sugar
50 g/2 oz rolled oats

To make the crumble topping, mix together the flour and salt and rub in the butter with your fingers to resemble breadcrumbs. Stir in the sugar and oats.

Mix together the apples, pears and raspberries in a suitable ovenproof dish (I use a 25 x 20 cm/10 x 8 inch oval dish), sprinkle over the sugar and top with the crumble mixture. Bake in an oven preheated to 200°C/400°F/Gas 6 for 30–35 minutes, by which time the top of the crumble should have turned a golden brown.

American-Style Cheesecake

This is one of the most delicious cheesecakes I have ever tasted. Serve it plain or with the cherry topping.

MAKES 10 ADULT PORTIONS

Base
250 g/9 oz digestive biscuits
125 g/4½ oz butter

Filling
225 g/8 oz caster sugar
3 tablespoons cornflour
675 g/1½ lb cream cheese, e.g.
Philadelphia

2 eggs
1 teaspoon vanilla essence or grated zest
of ½ lemon
300 ml/10 fl oz whipping cream
75 g/3 oz sultanas (optional)

Topping
425 g/15 oz canned cherries in syrup
½ tablespoon cornflour

To make the base, break the biscuits into pieces, put them in a plastic bag and crush with a rolling pin. Melt the butter and stir in the crushed biscuits. Line a 23 cm/9 inch springform cake tin with baking paper and grease the sides. Press the crushed biscuit mixture over the base.

For the filling, mix the sugar and cornflour. Beat in the cream cheese. Add the eggs and vanilla (or lemon zest). Beat until smooth. Slowly whisk in the cream until thickened. Stir in the sultanas. Pour over the biscuit base. Bake for 1 hour in an oven preheated to 180°C/350°F/Gas 4. Cool.

For the topping, drain the cherries, reserving 120 ml/4 fl oz syrup. Mix the cornflour with 1 tablespoon syrup. Pour the remaining syrup into a saucepan, stir in the cornflour mixture and bring to the boil, stirring until thick. Cool. Decorate the cheesecake with circles of cherries and pour over the glaze.

Iced Lollies

Iced lollies are always popular with children. You can buy lolly moulds with reusable plastic sticks. Fill the moulds with your chosen fruit purée or fruit juice, put the plastic sticks on top (these also serve as covers) and freeze on a level surface in the freezer. Dip the mould into warm water when you want to get an iced lolly out.

You can make your own fruit purées from fresh fruits in season or you can use natural fruit juices as the basis of your lollies. Experiment with different combinations like puréed and strained berry fruits sweetened with a little icing sugar mixed with blackcurrant juice, and stir in natural or fruit flavoured yoghurt for a frozen-yoghurt lolly. These pure ingredients are much better for your child than commercial iced lollies, many of which are full of additives, colourings and sugar.

My son Nicholas, when two years old, had fairly sophisticated taste and developed a penchant for passion-fruit ice lollies (as did his father, who goes straight for the freezer after supper!). Try also cranberry and raspberry juice or puréed canned lychees.

Two-tone iced lollies are fun. Half-fill the moulds with purée or juice of one colour, freeze, then pour over a purée of a contrasting colour.

Peach and Passion-Fruit Lollies

MAKES 6 ICED LOLLIES

*2 large oranges, squeezed
strained juice of 3 passion fruit*

*2 juicy ripe peaches, skinned, stoned and
chopped*

Combine all the ingredients in a blender or processor and blend until smooth. Pour into iced-lolly moulds and freeze.

Annabel's Bread and Butter Pudding

This is the perfect pudding for when the cupboard is pretty bare. It is also delicious made with raisin bread, cholla or sliced panettone cake.

MAKES 5 ADULT PORTIONS

250 ml/8 fl oz milk
250 ml/8 fl oz whipping cream
1 split vanilla pod
4 thin slices white bread, crusts removed
butter for spreading

50 g/2 oz sultanas
25 g/1 oz raisins
3 eggs
50 g/2 oz caster sugar
2 tablespoons apricot jam

Slowly boil the milk and cream in a saucepan with the vanilla pod, then remove from the heat. Stand for 10 minutes, then strain. Spread the bread with butter and cut each slice into four triangles. Arrange in a greased ovenproof dish (about 25 x 20 cm/10 x 8 inches) with the sultanas and raisins between the slices. Whisk the eggs with the sugar, then gradually mix in the milk and cream. Pour over the bread and bake in an oven pre-heated to 160°C/325°F/Gas 3 for 45–50 minutes. Remove and allow to cool a little. Gently heat the jam, with a little water, strain and brush over the pudding.

Grandma's Lokshen Pudding

Lokshen is vermicelli: very fine egg noodles.

MAKES 4 ADULT PORTIONS

225 g/8 oz vermicelli
1 large egg, beaten
25 g/1 oz butter, melted
250 ml/8 fl oz milk

1 tablespoon vanilla sugar or caster sugar
½ teaspoon mixed spice
75 g/3 oz each sultanas and raisins
a few flaked almonds (optional)

Cook the vermicelli in boiling water for about 5 minutes. Drain and mix with the remaining ingredients. Place in a greased, shallow baking dish, and bake in an oven preheated to 180°C/350°F/Gas 4 for about 30 minutes.

Frozen Strawberry Yoghurt
Ice Cream

A delicious easy-to-make frozen-yoghurt ice cream using only natural ingredients. You can also make a peach melba frozen yoghurt using fresh raspberries, puréed and strained, and peach yoghurt. I like to serve this as a Knickerbocker Glory in a tall glass with fresh berries.

MAKES 6 ADULT PORTIONS

100 g/4 oz caster sugar *300 ml/10 fl oz strawberry yoghurt*
300 ml/10 fl oz water *150 ml/5 fl oz double cream, whipped*
350 g/12 oz fresh strawberries *1 egg white, whisked*

Put the sugar in a saucepan with the water, bring to the boil and continue to boil for 5 minutes to make a syrup. Set aside to cool for a few minutes. Purée the strawberries and press through a sieve, then mix with the syrup and stir in the yoghurt and whipped cream. Churn for 10 minutes in an ice cream-making machine, then fold in the whipped egg white and churn for another 10 minutes or until firm.

This can also be made without an ice-cream-making machine but it will be more time-consuming. Pour the mixture into a freezerproof plastic container and freeze. Remove and whisk when semi-frozen, then return to the freezer. Whisk again after 1 hour, fold in the whipped egg white, freeze again and whisk twice more during the freezing process.

BAKING FOR TODDLERS
Funny Shape Biscuits

These biscuits contain no sugar and are ideal for babies who are teething. Biscuit cutters come in all sorts of weird and wonderful shapes. I use a gingerbread-man cutter and animal cut-outs and my son can't wait to get his hands on the biscuits. I get a running commentary as to which piece of the anatomy he has just eaten!

MAKES 15–20 BISCUITS (DEPENDING ON SIZE OF CUTTERS)

50 g/2 oz wholemeal flour
100 g/4 oz plain white flour
75 g/3 oz semolina
¼ teaspoon each ground ginger,
cinnamon and salt
75 g/3 oz margarine or butter

1 medium ripe banana
2 tablespoons maple syrup
1 egg, lightly beaten
cream cheese for spreading (optional)
a few raisins (optional)

Put the flours, semolina, ginger, cinnamon and salt into a mixing bowl and rub in the margarine or butter. Mash the banana well with the maple syrup and stir into the mixture to make a smooth pliable dough.

Roll out on lightly floured surface and cut into shapes with biscuit cutters. Brush with the beaten egg and bake on lightly greased baking trays in an oven preheated to 200°C/400°F/Gas 6 for 20 minutes until golden and firm. Cool on a wire rack.

If you wish, spread the cooled biscuits with cream cheese, marking with a fork to represent the animals' fur. Use pieces of raisin for eyes and noses.

Apple Flowers

You can use ready-rolled sheets of puff pastry, which only need to be unrolled and baked – so it couldn't be simpler to make these delicious pastries. Alternatively, use a block of puff pastry and roll it out yourself.

MAKES 6 MINI APPLE TARTS

300 g/11 oz puff pastry
40 g/1½ oz butter
40 g/1½ oz caster sugar
1 egg
a few drops of almond essence
50 g/2 oz ground almonds

25 g/1 oz melted butter
3 small eating apples
caster sugar for sprinkling
2 tablespoons apricot jam, strained
1 tablespoon lemon juice
6 glacé cherries

Preheat the oven to 200°C/400°F/Gas 6. Cut 6 circles out of the pastry using a round pastry cutter (approx. 10 cm/4 inches) or cut around a plate using a sharp knife. To make the almond filling, cream together the butter and sugar until soft, then beat in the egg, a few drops of almond essence and the ground almonds to make a smooth cream. Prick the pastry a few times with a fork and brush with a little melted butter. Spread some of the almond cream over each of the circles.

Peel and core the apples, then cut in half and slice thinly. Arrange the sliced fruit around the pastry circles. Brush with a little melted butter, sprinkle over some caster sugar and bake in the preheated oven for about 20 minutes or until the pastry is crisp and the fruit is cooked. Transfer the tarts to a wire rack to cool.

Warm the jam and lemon juice in a small saucepan and then brush the fruit with a little of the melted, strained apricot jam to glaze the tarts. Decorate the centre of each tart with a glacé cherry.

Smartie Fairy Cakes

These little cakes can be frozen, which is best done before they are iced.
They are ideal for a birthday celebration and it's fun to decorate them
with faces using sweets and tubes of writing icing.

MAKES 12 CAKES

100 g/4 oz soft margarine
100 g/4 oz caster sugar
2 eggs
100 g/4 oz self-raising flour
1 teaspoon vanilla essence

Cream-Cheese Icing
50 g/2 oz unsalted butter
225 g/8 oz icing sugar, sieved
1 teaspoon vanilla essence
100 g/4 oz cream cheese

Glacé Icing
225g/8 oz icing sugar, sieved
about 2 tablespoons water
a few drops of food colouring

Decoration
1 packet candy-coated chocolate
beans (Smarties)
1 packet dolly mixtures
assorted colours of writing icing
in tubes

Chocolate Icing
50 g/2 oz soft unsalted butter
75 g/3 oz icing sugar, sieved
1 tablespoon cocoa powder

Cream the margarine and sugar together until light and fluffy, then beat in the eggs one at a time together with 1 tablespoon of the flour. Add the vanilla essence and fold in the remaining flour. Line a bun tin with paper cases and half-fill each case with the mixture. Bake in an oven preheated to 180°C/350°F/Gas 4 for 20 minutes. Remove and cool on a wire rack.

I like to make two different coloured icings, so I use chocolate and then a pale cream-cheese icing. If you prefer, make a simple glacé icing. Mix the icing sugar with enough water to form a spreading consistency, then divide into two before you stir in the colouring, using different colours for each half.

For the chocolate icing, cut the butter into small pieces and beat it in a bowl with a wooden spoon until creamy. Beat the sugar a little at a time into the butter, then beat in the cocoa powder.

For the cream-cheese icing, beat the butter, sugar and vanilla essence until crumbly. Stir in the cream cheese. Do not over-beat or it will become watery. Spread over the cakes.

Ice and decorate the cakes with funny faces.

Pineapple and Raisin Muffins

These are absolutely delicious, and very healthy too; they never last long in our house!

MAKES ABOUT 13 MUFFINS

100 g/4 oz plain flour
100 g/4 oz plain wholemeal flour
1 teaspoon baking powder
¾ teaspoon bicarbonate of soda
1 teaspoon ground cinnamon
1 teaspoon ground ginger
½ teaspoon salt

175 ml/6 fl oz vegetable oil
75 g/3 oz caster sugar
2 eggs
125 g/4½ oz grated carrots
225 g/8 oz canned crushed pineapple, drained
100 g/4 oz raisins

Preheat the oven to 180°C/350°F/Gas 4. Sift together the flours, baking powder, bicarbonate of soda, cinnamon, ginger and salt and mix well. Beat the oil, sugar and eggs together until well blended. Add the grated carrots, crushed pineapple and raisins. Gradually add the flour mixture, beating just enough to combine all the ingredients.

Pour the batter into muffin trays lined with paper cases and bake for about 25 minutes or until golden. (These can be cooked in fairy-cake trays, but you will need to reduce the cooking time.) Cool on a wire rack.

Yoghurt Magimix Cake

This cake has a lovely flavour and a very moist texture. It takes no more than 5 minutes to prepare. You can also make it in two sandwich tins. Beat 250 ml/8 fl oz double cream with 25 g/1 oz caster sugar and fold in 100 g/4 oz raspberries, and use this to sandwich the two cakes together.

MAKES 8 ADULT PORTIONS

160 g/5¼ oz caster sugar
250 ml/8 fl oz vegetable oil
225 ml/8 fl oz natural set yoghurt
2 eggs

225 g/8 oz plain flour
3 teaspoons baking powder
2 teaspoons vanilla essence
icing sugar

Grease a 25 cm/10 inch round chiffon cake tin. In a blender or food processor, mix the sugar with the oil, then add the yoghurt and mix. Blend with the eggs, flour, baking powder and vanilla essence. Pour into the prepared tin and bake in an oven preheated to 160°C/325°F/Gas 3 for about 50 minutes. Sift icing sugar over the top when cold.

White-Chocolate-Button Cookies

These are so easy to make and are really delicious. Baked for only 12 minutes, they should be quite soft when they are taken out of the oven so that when they cool down they are lovely and moist.

MAKES 20 COOKIES

100 g/4 oz unsalted butter or margarine at room temperature
100 g/4 oz caster sugar
100 g/4 oz brown sugar
1 egg
1 teaspoon vanilla essence

175 g/6 oz plain flour
½ teaspoon baking powder
¼ teaspoon salt
175 g/6 oz white chocolate buttons
75 g/3 oz pecans or walnuts, chopped (optional)

Beat the butter or margarine together with the sugars. With a fork, beat the egg together with the vanilla and add this to the butter mixture.

In a bowl, mix together the flour, baking powder and salt. Add this to the butter and egg mixture and blend well.

Break the chocolate buttons into smaller pieces with a rolling pin or in a food processor, and stir these, together with the nuts (if using), into the mixture.

Line several baking sheets with non-stick baking paper and roll the dough into walnut-sized balls. Put these onto the sheets, spaced well apart, and bake in an oven preheated to 190°C/375°F/Gas 5 for 12 minutes. Take carefully off the baking paper and let them cool.

My Favourite Chocolate Biscuit Squares

These are great for a children's party or tea-time treat.

MAKES 16 CHOCOLATE BISCUIT SQUARES

100 g/4 oz digestive biscuits
100 g/4 oz ginger biscuits
150 g/5 oz milk chocolate
100 g/4 oz plain chocolate
85 g/3 oz golden syrup

85 g/3 oz unsalted butter
100 g/4 oz ready-to-eat dried apricots, chopped
50 g/2 oz raisins
40 g/1½ oz Rice Krispies

Lightly grease and line a 20 cm/8 inch square shallow tin. Break the biscuits, place in a plastic bag and crush with a rolling pin to form coarse crumbs.

Melt the chocolate, syrup and butter in a heatproof bowl over a saucepan of simmering water. Stir in the biscuit crumbs until well coated, then add the chopped apricots and raisins and, finally, stir in the Rice Krispies.

Spoon the mixture into the prepared tin. Level the surface, pressing down with a masher, and put in the fridge to set. Cut into squares before serving.

Traditional English Fruit Cake

I like to make several of these dark rich fruit cakes with my children a month before Christmas as presents for teachers, family and friends. We decorate them and put them in fancy cake tins; they will keep well for several months. If making this for adults, soak the fruit in brandy and port instead of orange juice – it tastes wonderful. For added flavour, make holes in the cake with a skewer and add extra brandy and port after the cake is cooked.

MAKES 16 ADULT PORTIONS

150 ml / 5 fl oz orange juice or
4 tablespoons each brandy and port
275 g / 10 oz each currants and sultanas
350 g / 12 oz raisins
225 g / 8 oz plain flour
1 teaspoon baking powder
½ teaspoon salt
2 teaspoons ground cinnamon
1 teaspoon ground ginger
2 teaspoons mixed spice

225 g / 8 oz butter
150 g / 5 oz brown sugar
4 eggs
150 g / 5 oz mixed peel
100 g / 4 oz glacé cherries, chopped
100 g / 4 oz pecans or walnuts, chopped
100 g / 4 oz apricot jam
3 tablespoons water
extra pecans or walnuts and glacé fruits
for decoration

Pour the orange juice over the dried fruit and leave to soak overnight. Sift together the flour, baking powder, salt and spices. Cream the butter with the sugar. Beat in the eggs, one at a time, with 1 tablespoon of the flour mixture. Stir in the remaining flour mixture and the dried fruit, peel, cherries and nuts. Line the base of a 25 cm / 10 inch round cake tin and grease the sides. Pour in the cake mix. Bake in an oven preheated to 150°C / 300°F / Gas 2 for 2–2½ hours. If the top is getting too brown, cover with greaseproof paper. When cooked, a skewer inserted into the centre of the cake should come out clean. Cool in the tin for 30 minutes. Turn out onto a wire rack to cool thoroughly. Wrap in foil and store in a cool dry place.

Warm the jam and water and press through a sieve. Brush the top of the cake with some glaze and decorate with the fruit and nuts. Brush with the remaining glaze.

Cheese Pretzels

These are delicious and great fun to make. Your children will enjoy helping you twist the pretzels into different shapes. You can even make letters of the alphabet and spell your child's name.

MAKES 20 PRETZELS

1 sachet dried yeast
225 ml / 8 fl oz warm water
350 g / 12 oz plain flour
½ teaspoon salt

150 g / 5 oz Gruyère or Cheddar cheese, grated
2 tablespoons vegetable oil
1 tablespoon sea salt
1 tablespoon sesame seeds

Dissolve the yeast in the warm water. Sift the flour and salt into a large bowl and stir in the cheese, oil and yeast liquid. Bring together to form a dough and knead on a floured surface for 10 minutes by hand, or for 5 minutes using a dough hook. Place in an oiled bowl, cover with clingfilm and leave in a warm place for about 1 hour. Break off small pieces of dough, roll into 25 cm / 10 inch long strands and twist into pretzel shapes. Arrange on a greased baking tray. Brush with oil and sprinkle some with sea salt and some with sesame seeds. Bake in an oven preheated to 200°C/400°F/Gas 6 for 15 minutes until golden brown.

HEALTHY SNACKS

Fruit Snacks

Wash fruit well. Peel, core, deseed or stone and trim as needed.

Bananas, whole or cut into pieces

Chunks of peeled and cored apples

Chunks of pear

Orange, mandarin or clementine segments with as much of the pith removed as possible (make sure there are no pips in the fruit)

Kiwi fruit, peeled and sliced

Strawberries, hulled and halved

Seedless grapes, skinned for babies under one year

Melon, peeled and cut into bite-sized pieces

Peaches, skinned and sliced

Mango, peeled and sliced

Papaya, peeled, deseeded and cut in thick slices

Raspberries, carefully washed

Lychees, peeled and stoned (toddlers can easily choke on lychee stones)

Pineapple, peeled and cut into chunks

Dried fruit such as apricots, prunes, raisins (if too tough, soak in boiling water)

Chocolate-Dipped Fruit

A very appealing way of giving fruit to children is to melt some dark chocolate in a double boiler (or a microwave), dip the tip of the fruit piece into the chocolate and pierce the fruit with a cocktail stick. Stick the cocktail sticks with the fruit into an orange and put this into the fridge to allow the chocolate to harden. Strawberries, pineapple chunks and orange or tangerine segments are especially nice. Remember to remove the cocktail sticks before giving the fruit to your child.

Whole bananas can be coated in chocolate. Place on greaseproof paper and freeze or chill until the chocolate has set.

If you are worried about your child having too much chocolate, use carob as a substitute.

SNACKS THAT WON'T HARM YOUR CHILD'S TEETH

Vegetable Snacks

As with fruit, wash, peel, trim and deseed as appropriate.

Toddlers love to dip raw vegetable sticks into a sauce, and a nicely arranged selection of crudités is great for a toddler who is teething. You can buy packs of peeled mini carrots in the supermarket, and these are ideal for toddlers, as are strips of red pepper, sugar snap peas, cucumber sticks and cherry tomatoes. Try giving your child some simple but delicious dips like the Green Goddess Dip (see page 182), or make one by combining soured cream or cream cheese, a little ketchup, some chives and seasoning. You can also buy ready-made dips such as *hummous* made from chickpeas – which is very nutritious.

Carrots and white cabbage, grated and mixed with a little mayonnaise and raisins, make a simple and nutritious snack piled onto lettuce leaves.

Cheese Snacks

Cheese makes an ideal snack for toddlers. Try using a biscuit cutter to make animal shapes from slices of cheese. Edam, Gruyère and Emmenthal are particular favourites with most children. Individual cheeses like the small round Babybel and the wrapped triangles of cheese are ideal as well.

Cottage cheese is also popular, plain or simply mixed with something like chopped pineapple. You could also make a scoopful of cheese into a ball, accompany it with a scoopful of grated apple mixed with raisins, and surround it with a selection of mixed fruit chopped very small. This makes a nutritious, yet delicious, snack.

Green Goddess Dip

Serve this tasty dip surrounded by a selection of raw vegetable sticks like carrots, cucumber, red pepper and celery. Add some cherry tomatoes, corn chips and breadsticks for a popular and nutritious snack.

MAKES 2 ADULT PORTIONS

1 large ripe avocado
½ tablespoon fresh lemon juice
2 tablespoons cream cheese
1 tablespoon sliced spring onion

2 tomatoes, skinned, deseeded and finely chopped
1 tablespoon diced sweet red pepper
salt and pepper to taste

Cut the avocado in half, stone and scoop the flesh out of the skin. Mash it together with the rest of the ingredients. This will turn brown if left standing for too long.

Chef's Salad with Turkey and Cheese

MAKES 3 CHILD PORTIONS

Dressing
3 tablespoons light olive oil
1 tablespoon runny honey
1 tablespoon soy sauce
1½ tablespoons freshly squeezed lemon juice

1 little gem lettuce, cut into small pieces
2 medium tomatoes (250 g / 9 oz), skinned, deseeded and chopped
125 g / 4½ oz cooked turkey or chicken, diced
60 g / 2½ oz Edam cheese, cubed or cooked pasta
100 g / 4 oz canned sweetcorn

Whisk together all the ingredients for the dressing. Put the rest of the ingredients into a bowl and toss together with the dressing.

Home-Made Fast-Food Pizza

These delicious easy-to-make pizzas are always popular. If you prefer, you can use crumpets or small baguettes cut in half as an alternative to the muffin bases.

MAKES 4 MINI PIZZAS

1 spring onion, finely sliced
4 button mushrooms, washed and sliced
15 g/½ oz butter
2 tomatoes, skinned, deseeded and chopped
1 dessertspoon tomato purée

1 dessertspoon fresh basil, chopped
50 g/2 oz frozen sweetcorn
a little freshly ground black pepper
2 English muffins, split in half
40 g/1½ oz Cheddar cheese, grated

Sauté the spring onion and mushrooms in the butter for 2 minutes. Stir in the tomatoes, tomato purée and basil and cook for 2 minutes more. Cook the sweetcorn according to the packet instructions, combine it with the tomato mixture and season with a little pepper. Heat the grill and toast the split muffins for a few minutes. Top with the tomato and sweetcorn mixture, sprinkle with the grated cheese and grill until the cheese is bubbling and golden.

Stuffed Eggs

Cut hard-boiled eggs in half lengthways and cut a thin sliver off the base of each half so that they stand firm. Finely mash the yolks with one of the following, and fill the hollow. Remember that the hollow of a boiled egg is quite small, so you do not need a lot of filling.

chopped cucumber, lettuce, tomato, and mayonnaise
OR
cottage cheese and chives
OR
poached salmon and mayonnaise

OR
finely chopped chicken and tomato ketchup
OR
canned salmon or tuna, mayonnaise and chopped spring onion

Top-Hat Egg

This is a great snack or breakfast treat for children and they'll have fun helping you make it. You could also use biscuit cutters to cut out shapes like a heart or an animal in the centre of the bread.

MAKES 1 ADULT PORTION

1 thick slice bread
15 g/½ oz butter

1 egg yolk
salt and pepper

Press out a circle from the centre of the bread using a pastry cutter of about 7½ cm/3 inch diameter. Butter both sides of the bread and fry on one side for about 1 minute in a small frying pan. Flip the bread over, place a knob of butter in the hole and allow it to sizzle. Crack the egg into the hole, season lightly and cook, covered, for about 4 minutes or until set. Serve with the circle of fried bread over the egg.

On-the-Go Snacks

When you are out and about or going on a journey with your toddler, it's a good idea to fill a small plastic container or sandwich bag with a selection of healthy snacks for little fingers to delve into and nibble when they feel peckish.

Fresh fruit like grapes, satsumas, blueberries, bananas, plums or cherries make an ideal snack for young children. Ready-to-eat dried fruits also make nutritious snacks, e.g. mini boxes of raisins, yoghurt raisins, apricots, apple rings, mango, dates, figs, prunes or banana chips.

For something more savoury, give mini cheeses, cherry tomatoes, cucumber or carrot sticks.

You could also offer your child's favourite healthy breakfast cereals, or popcorn, mini rice cakes or mini sandwiches, e.g. Marmite or Peanut butter.

Sandwiches

Sandwiches can come in all shapes and sizes. Try making animal-shaped sandwiches by cutting them out with a biscuit cutter. Pinwheel sandwiches are very appealing too (see page 186).

Toasted sandwiches are a meal in themselves. It is well worth investing in a toasted-sandwich maker that seals the bread.

Try experimenting with lots of different types of bread: small round pitta breads slit and stuffed with salad; raisin bread; open sandwiches on bridge rolls; bagels (these are excellent for a toddler to chew on when he is teething); tortilla wraps; French bread; or even a simple sandwich with one side made from white bread and the other brown.

Presentation is very important. A child is far more likely to eat something that looks appealing. Sprinkle the sandwiches with salad cress, decorate with thinly serrated vegetables or make your sandwiches into little trains or boats. It doesn't take long and it's fun to do. I think you will find that a lot of toddlers will reach out for your sandwiches.

On the following pages are some suggestions for sandwich fillings. Your toddler will soon let you know his preferences!

Pinwheel Sandwiches

Remove the crusts from two slices of bread. Place them on a board, over-lapping the edges slightly, and then roll them together with a rolling pin to join the slices together and gently flatten the bread, making it more pliable. Alternatively, cut the crust from the side of a long rectangular dense-textured loaf, and cut into long thin slices – this way you can prepare pinwheels without any join. Spread evenly with butter or mar-garine and the desired filling, and roll up the bread like a Swiss roll. Cut into slices to make little pin-wheels. It is a good idea to prepare these in advance, wrap them in cling film and set aside in the fridge – they will slice better if chilled first.

You can even make a variegated pinwheel sandwich by rolling one brown and one white slice of bread (spread with different but comple-mentary fillings) together.

Chocolate spread and banana
Peanut butter and raspberry jam
Peanut butter and mashed banana
Cream cheese and ham
Smoked salmon
Cream cheese and crushed
    pineapple (or fruit purée)

Peanuts can cause allergic reactions (see page 15).

Cream or curd cheese, toasted sesame seeds, and mustard and cress

Cream cheese and cucumber

Cream cheese and crushed cornflakes

Cream cheese and strawberry jam in raisin bread

Cream cheese with slices of smoked salmon in a bagel

Cream cheese with chopped dried apricots

Cream cheese and redcurrant jelly

Cottage cheese with avocado and lemon juice

Cheese and chutney

Grated cheese and carrot with mayonnaise

Plain fromage frais and raisins

Taramasalata

Sliced falafel with grated carrots and raisins

Chopped hard-boiled egg, watercress and mayonnaise

Egg mayonnaise with a little curry powder

Chopped hard-boiled egg with mashed sardines

Tuna mayonnaise and salad cress

Tuna or salmon with sweetcorn, spring onion and mayonnaise

Canned salmon, chopped egg and mayonnaise

Chopped chicken, mayonnaise and yoghurt with a little curry powder and raisins

Chicken or turkey with chutney

Bacon, lettuce, tomato and a little mayonnaise

Open Toasted Sandwiches

Toast the bread, spread with the topping and cook under a hot grill.

Cheese and tomato

Diced ham and pineapple with grated cheese

Canned sardines in tomato sauce

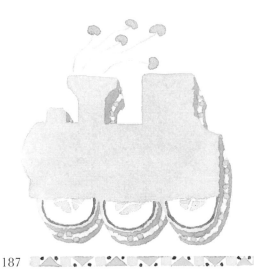

TODDLER MEAL PLANNER

	Breakfast	*Lunch*	*Dinner*
Day 1	**Fruity Swiss Muesli,** Yoghurt Fruit	**Annabel's Tasty Beefburgers** with vegetables **Pear, Apple and Raspberry Crumble** with custard	**Two Tomato Pasta Sauce Frozen Strawberry Yoghurt Ice Cream**
Day 2	Cheese on toast **Apricot, Apple and Pear Custard**	**Grandma's Tasty Fish Pie** Fruit	**Chicken Fillets with Mango Chutney and Apricots** with vegetables **Poached Fruits**
Day 3	Porridge with honey or jam Apple purée *Petit Suisse*	**Marinated Chicken on the Griddle** with vegetables and chips **Annabel's Bread and Butter Pudding**	**Bow-Ties with Gruyère and Cherry Tomatoes** Fruit and ice cream
Day 4	Scrambled eggs Cereal Fruit	**Chicken and Apple Balls Snow-Covered Fruit Salad**	**Nursery Fish Pie Home-Made Fruit Jelly**
Day 5	**Pineapple and Raisin Muffins** Yoghurt Fruit	**Shepherd's Pie** with vegetables **Strawberry Rice Pudding**	**Spaghetti Primavera** Fruit
Day 6	Boiled eggs with fingers of toast Prunes Yoghurt	**Toasted Tuna Muffins Home-Made Fruit Jelly**	**Bow-Ties with Tomato and Mozzarella Sauce** Fruit and ice-cream
Day 7	Cereal Cheese Fruit	**Chef's Salad with Turkey and Cheese Pear, Apple and Raspberry Crumble**	**Tuna Tagliatelle Peaches with Amaretti Biscuits**

These meal charts show you how to plan ahead and cook for the whole family together.

FAMILY MEAL PLANNER

	Breakfast	Lunch	Dinner
Day 1	**Fruity Swiss Muesli** Yoghurt	**Annabel's Hidden-Vegetable Tomato Sauce** with chicken and rice	**Annabel's Tasty Beefburgers** with vegetables and potato **Pear, Apple and Raspberry Crumble** with custard
Day 2	**My Favourite Pancakes Apricot, Apple and Pear Custard**	**Chicken and Apple Balls** with vegetables	**Grandma's Tasty Fish Pie** with vegetables **Snow-Covered Fruit Salad**
Day 3	**French Toast Cut-Outs** Baked beans	**Tuna and Sweetcorn Stuffed Potato** Fruit	**Marinated Chicken on the Griddle** and **Special Fried Rice Frozen Strawberry Yoghurt Ice Cream** or yoghurt and fruit
Day 4	Scrambled egg Cereal	**Thai-Style Chicken and Noodles** Fruit salad	**My Favourite Pasta with Broccoli Home-Made Fruit Jelly** and ice cream
Day 5	**Pineapple and Raisin Muffins** Yoghurt and honey	**Cod in a Cheese Sauce with Matchstick Vegetables**	**Shepherd's Pie** with vegetables or salad **Poached Fruits**
Day 6	**The Three Bears' Breakfast** Prunes	**Toasted Tuna Muffins** Fruit	**Mini Minute Steaks** with potato **Home-Made Fruit Jelly** and ice cream
Day 7	**Cheese Scramble** and toast Fruit	**Stir-Fried Chicken** or **Bar-B-Q Chicken** with vegetables **Annabel's Bread and Butter Pudding**	**Gratin of Sole Ratatouille with Rice or Pasta**

INDEX

ACKNOWLEDGEMENTS

I am indebted to the following people for their help and advice during the writing of this book.

Dr Stephen Herman FRCP, Consultant Paediatrician, Central Middlesex Hospital.
Margaret Lawson, Senior Lecturer in Paediatric Nutrition, Institute of Child Health.
Professor Charles Brook, Consultant Paediatric Endocrinologist, Middlesex Hospital.
Dr Sam Tucker FRCP, Consultant Paediatrician, Hillingdon Hospital.
Jacky Bernett, Community Dietician.
Dr Tim Lobstein, specialist in children's food and nutrition at The London Food Commission.
Carol Nock SRN FCN, Midwife.
Kathy Morgan, State Registered Health Visitor.
My mother, Evelyn Etkind, for all her encouragement in writing this book.
David Karmel, for his patience in teaching me how to use a computer.
Beryl Lewsey, for her enthusiasm and hard work.
Ros Edwards, Ian Jackson, Susan Fleming, Fiona Eves and Elaine Partington of Eddison Sadd.
Dr Irving Etkind, for his help in research.
Jane Hamilton, my nanny, for restraining my children from wiping out my manuscript on the computer!
And, most important of all, my husband Simon, my chief guinea pig, for all his support.

The Author

Annabel Karmel is a leading author on cooking for children. After the death of her first child, who died of a rare viral disease aged just under three months, Annabel wrote *The Complete Baby and Toddler Meal Planner*, which is now an international bestseller. She has written ten other books including *Superfoods For Babies and Children*, *The Complete First Year Planner* and *Annabel Karmel's Family Meal Planner*.

Annabel lives in London and is the mother of three children, Nicholas, Lara and Scarlett. As a trained cordon bleu cook and young mother, she experienced first-hand the difficulties in feeding young children. She thoroughly researched all aspects of feeding babies and children to cut through the often confusing and conflicting advice given to parents on the subject. She combined her findings with her own experience and knowledge of cooking, testing each recipe on a panel of babies and toddlers.

Annabel appears frequently on television and writes regularly for magazines and newspapers, including *The Times*, *Prima Baby*, *BBC Parenting*, *Baby and You* and *Bella* magazine.

EDDISON·SADD EDITIONS

Editors   Fiona Eves, Susan Fleming and Katie Ginn
Proofreader   Kathy Steer
Indexer   Dorothy Frame
Art Director   Elaine Partington
Mac Designer   Brazzle Atkins
Production   Carol Anne Herron and Nick Eddison